The World's Greatest Churches

William R. Cook, Ph.D.

THE
GREAT
COURSES®

PUBLISHED BY:

THE GREAT COURSES
Corporate Headquarters
4840 Westfields Boulevard, Suite 500
Chantilly, Virginia 20151-2299
Phone: 1-800-832-2412
Fax: 703-378-3819
www.thegreatcourses.com

William R. Cook, Ph.D.
Distinguished Teaching Professor
of History Emeritus
State University of New York at Geneseo

Professor William R. Cook is Distinguished Teaching Professor of History Emeritus at the State University of New York at Geneseo (SUNY Geneseo), where he taught for 42 years. He holds an A.B. from Wabash College (cum laude, Phi Beta Kappa) and an M.A. and a Ph.D. from Cornell University. In 2010, he was awarded an honorary L.H.D. degree from his undergraduate alma mater. From 2008 to 2010 and again in 2013, he was Visiting Professor of History and Religion at Wabash College. He is a specialist in medieval and Renaissance history and the history of Christianity.

Professor Cook has focused his research for much of his career on Saint Francis of Assisi and the Franciscan Order. He is especially interested in how the art of the medieval and Renaissance periods teaches and informs those who see it. He also has done research on monasticism and, in collaboration with his colleague Ronald Herzman, has written and lectured about Dante and his *Divine Comedy*. Professor Cook is a frequent speaker at Renaissance Weekends and, for the past five years, has spoken on religion and democracy at Forum 2000 in Prague. In recent years, he has expanded his study of Christianity to focus on how Christianity is practiced and thought about beyond Europe and North America and has traveled throughout the world to experience Christianity in different cultural and political settings.

Professor Cook received the Chancellor's Award for Excellence in Teaching in 1974 and was named SUNY Distinguished Teaching Professor in 1984. In 1992, he was named Professor of the Year for the state of New York by the Council for Advancement and Support of Education. In 2004, he was runner-up for the Robert Foster Cherry Award for Great Teaching at Baylor University. With Ronald Herzman, he was named the first recipient of the CARA Award for Excellence in Teaching Medieval Studies by the Medieval Academy of America.

Professor Cook has led study tours and taught courses in Europe, especially in Italy, for 40 years and recently took a group of Wabash College students to Kenya to study Christianity there. He also has traveled with individual students to conduct research in many countries in Europe, as well as in Peru and the Philippines. He regularly does programs for Friends of Florence and has led alumni tours for both SUNY Geneseo and Wabash. He has spoken to the Young Presidents' Organization and CEO (another organization of CEOs) in Italy, France, Ireland, Spain, the Czech Republic, Greece, Turkey, and Japan. He is also a frequent speaker at academic conferences and recently keynoted a conference on Franciscan art in Genoa, Italy.

Professor Cook has authored a number of books, including *Francis of Assisi: The Way of Poverty and Humility*; *Francis in America: A Catalog of Early Paintings of St. Francis of Assisi in the United States and Canada*; and *Images of St Francis of Assisi in Painting, Stone and Glass from the Earliest Images to Ca. 1320 in Italy: A Catalogue*. He also has edited a book of essays entitled *The Art of the Franciscan Order in Italy*. In addition, Professor Cook has appeared in television documentaries about both Dante and Saint Francis—in particular, the acclaimed *Reluctant Saint: Francis of Assisi* the Hallmark Channel.

For The Great Courses, Professor Cook has taught *The Cathedral*; *The Catholic Church: A History*; *Tocqueville and the American Experiment*; *The Lives of Great Christians*; *Machiavelli in Context*; and with Ronald Herzman, *Dante's Divine Comedy*, *Francis of Assisi*, and *St. Augustine's Confessions*. ∎

Table of Contents

INTRODUCTION

Professor Biography i
Course Scope 1

LECTURE GUIDES

LECTURE 1
The Earliest Churches 3

LECTURE 2
The Church of the Holy Sepulchre 11

LECTURE 3
Hagia Sophia 18

LECTURE 4
The Cave Churches of Cappadocia 25

LECTURE 5
Great Churches of Russia 31

LECTURE 6
The Painted Churches of Romania 37

LECTURE 7
The Churches of Armenia 45

LECTURE 8
The Churches of Georgia 53

LECTURE 9
The Rock-Hewn Churches of Ethiopia 59

LECTURE 10
The Mosque-Cathedral of Córdoba 66

Table of Contents

LECTURE 11
The Stave Churches of Norway..72

LECTURE 12
The Pilgrimage Church of Sainte-Foy 79

LECTURE 13
The Cathedral of Monreale..86

LECTURE 14
Chartres Cathedral 92

LECTURE 15
Winchester Cathedral 98

LECTURE 16
The Cathedral of Siena..104

LECTURE 17
St. Peter's Basilica 110

LECTURE 18
The Wieskirche in Bavaria...117

LECTURE 19
La Compañía and Las Lajas Sanctuary 124

LECTURE 20
Guadalupe and the Cathedral of Mexico City.................131

LECTURE 21
Four Great American Churches......................................137

LECTURE 22
La Sagrada Família 145

LECTURE 23
Iceland's Hallgrímskirkja..152

Table of Contents

LECTURE 24
Two Churches in Seoul, Korea 160

SUPPLEMENTAL MATERIAL

Glossary 169
Bibliography 171
Notes 184

The World's Greatest Churches

Scope:

In Europe and the Americas, churches traditionally were and often still are prominent on skylines of great cities and remote villages. Their size and prominence suggest how important Christianity is or was for those places. In many instances, these buildings are also the most important sites for a visitor to see and places of civic pride. That is true in Paris, Moscow, Rio, and New Orleans but also for the Episcopal church in a small town in western New York because of its Tiffany windows or a village in southwestern Tuscany for its 12th-century Cistercian abbey.

In this course, we will consider what churches represent and give testimony to all over the world. The churches we will explore are large and small, urban and rural, old and new, and in one instance, unfinished. Some are elaborately decorated, while others are stunningly plain. Some are "must sees" for millions of travelers, while in others, the visitor may well be alone. We will examine churches on 5 continents and in 20 countries, from Colombia to South Korea and from Ethiopia to Iceland.

It is always important to look at the function of each church—a cathedral, monastery, shrine, or parish church. The reason for this is that a church is, first and foremost, a place where communities of Christians gather to worship, to give thanks, and to call on God for help. Thus, one way to judge the greatness of a church is to examine how well it serves its essential purpose. Our churches will range from one that proudly proclaims the power and splendor of the Roman Catholic Church and another the power and splendor of medieval Byzantium, to one that starkly requires us to experience Christ's Passion and death, to one that could be mistaken for a home and is known to its community as a meetinghouse.

Many churches are also in a real sense "schools" for teaching the essentials and traditions of the faith. This may simply be a building in the shape of a cross, but it often involves the use of paint, sculpted stone, stained glass, and other forms of decoration. In a Romanian church, we will discover a painting for each day of the year to be used as a calendar. At Chartres, we find narratives in stone and glass that teach profound theological lessons, as well as initiate believers to the traditions of the faith.

Churches also often serve civic functions. Hence, the Cathedral of Siena is a building that glorifies Siena almost as much as it glorifies God, and the same has been said of the National Cathedral in Washington, DC, and the Metropolitan Cathedral in Mexico City.

Churches that are shrines constantly welcome pilgrims. They come to visit the burial place of an important saint and, in the Holy Land, places associated with the life of Jesus. In significant ways, the act of pilgrims reaching their destination is a metaphor for the faithful taking a journey of faith, righting themselves when lost, finding encouragement when tired, and arriving at the goal because of perseverance.

It is important that we look at churches in places where Christianity has existed for a long time and where it is the dominant religion—not just in Europe but also in Armenia, Georgia, and Ethiopia—but it is equally important to examine churches that represent the experience of Christians in the Americas and in East Asia.

After examining some of the most beautiful buildings in the world, we will not only have more insight into masterpieces of architecture, painting, and sculpture but also a deeper understanding of the diversity of Christianity as expressed in its places of worship and an awareness that a church is in constant dialogue with the community it houses. ■

The Earliest Churches

Lecture 1

The Greek word that we translate as "church" is *ekklesia*, which can be more generally translated as "assembly." In other words, the basic meaning of the word *church* is not a building but an assembly of people. Throughout this course, as we look at both spectacular and simple buildings, we never want to forget that the essence of the word *church* is people: Churches were designed to hold communities of people. Thus, one of the questions we will ask is: How well does this building express the faith, values, culture, desires, and dreams of the people for whom it was built?

Obviously, in different places, times, and economies and with different groups of Christians who have different organizational principles and sets of beliefs within the large body of Christians, churches will look very different. A cathedral, for example, is a place for great ceremonies and the seat of a bishop's power. It will look quite different from a parish church, in part because it has a different function. Thus, function—along with the belief system and structure of a particular form of Christianity—is also important in defining a church.

Geography is important in this definition, as well. The early churches that we will explore are made primarily of stone and sometimes of wood. As we'll see, one way of looking at a church is through its building materials and the technology used in its construction. Poor communities or communities where Christians are a minority will not build large churches. In other words, the size of a church will differ depending on such simple factors as the economy or the number of people who will worship in it.

Generally speaking, churches didn't really exist until the 4th century. Before that time, most Christians worshipped at home, at least in part because within the Roman Empire, they sometimes experienced hostility or persecution. There is some archaeological evidence that in certain places and in more peaceful times in those first three centuries, there may have been some modest buildings built for Christian worship, but nothing very large and nothing that survives. Nevertheless, everything changed in the 4th century with the patronage of the emperor Constantine. By the beginning of the 5th century, Christianity was the official religion of the Roman Empire and probably the empire's majority religion. It's also important to note that Armenia, Georgia, and Ethiopia became Christian in the 4th century, as well, and we will look at churches in those places, representing different forms of Christianity.

Throughout this course, we will see churches built in the 4th century, one that is not yet complete, and many from time periods in between. We will see many different forms or denominations of Christianity. We will travel to five continents and will look at wonderful decorations in stone, glass, and paint; wooden objects; and even a holy book. As we explore these churches and objects, we will return to certain themes: How are the churches alike, and how and why are they different? How do they reflect and teach a particular community of people in a particular time, place, and culture? We will discuss the dialogue between the universal and the particular, and we will see how elements of preexisting and contemporary non-Christian cultures were woven into the fabric of Christianity and Christianized in the process. In this first lecture, we will learn why Christians wanted their churches to be different from pagan temples, and we'll look in particular at the basilica, the building form adopted by early Christians for their assemblies.

Suggested Reading

Krautheimer, *Early Christian and Byzantine Architecture*, parts I–III. These sections of the book deal with Christian buildings from the beginning through the 5th century.

Witcombe, *Art History Resources*. http://arthistoryresources.net/ARTHearlychristian.html#Top, From this page, you can look at the major early Christian churches of Rome, including many drawings and models of what those churches were like when they were built.

1. How does knowing that the word *church* refers to Christians rather than to the buildings in which they worship affect how we approach and understand these buildings? Try visiting several churches around you and see how they express what the Christian community identifies as its understanding of the faith.

2. Early Christians borrowed architectural and decorative elements from the paganism of the Roman Empire. What are the reasons for and possible pitfalls of doing this? How will thinking about this question prepare us for Christianity "to the ends of the earth" that we shall encounter in this course?

Amiens Cathedral.

© aladin56/iStock/Thinkstock.

Quaker meetinghouse, Pawling, NY; 18th century.

The Parthenon.

Basilica of St. Paul outside the Walls.

Santa Sabina, Rome.

Interior of Santa Sabina.

St. Euphrasius, Porec, Croatia; 6th century.

9

Mosaic, Church of Sant'Apollinare Ravenna, 6th century.

The Church of the Holy Sepulchre
Lecture 2

J esus was crucified about 30 C.E., but Christians often forget what happened in Palestine following the death of Jesus and his Resurrection. In 70 C.E., the city of Jerusalem was taken and largely destroyed by an army of the Roman Empire under the emperor Vespasian and his son Titus. Jerusalem lay in ruins for some time, but in 135, the emperor Hadrian decided to build a new Roman city there. This, of course, was at a time when Christianity was a minor and unrecognized religion of the empire. Once Constantine became the emperor, Christianity became the favored religion, and by the end of the 4th century, it was the official religion of the Roman Empire. At that time, Jerusalem took on a new meaning in the life of the empire.

Helena, the mother of Constantine, traveled to the Holy Land to seek out all the places that were associated with the life of Jesus. A particularly important event was the discovery of what she believed to be the Cross on which Jesus was crucified. On that site, she built the Church of the Holy Sepulchre.

Not surprisingly, the church that survives today does not resemble the structure that was built in the 4th century. In the 6th century, the Persians occupied Jerusalem, and in the 7th century, the Muslims conquered the area. There was a good deal of toleration, and the building remained intact during those periods, but it was more or less leveled around the year 1009. In fact, the destruction of the church was one of the major reasons for the calling of the First Crusade in 1095. The idea was to recapture the Holy Land to make it, once again, a place of Christian pilgrimage and to rebuild the Holy Sepulchre. In 1099, the rebuilding of the church began. At that time, many places outside the church that had been identified with Christ's Passion were incorporated into the church itself.

Today, six different denominations of Christianity have a space in the Holy Sepulchre: Egyptian, Syrian, Armenian, Greek Orthodox, Catholic, and Ethiopian Christians. Any changes at all in the Holy Sepulchre must be done with the unanimous agreement of these groups—which almost never agree on anything. Thus, in many ways, the Church of the Holy Sepulchre is not only a holy place for all Christians, but it also represents the fact that different kinds of Christians can live together—although not always as peacefully and as lovingly as we might expect. In many ways—and quite properly—the Church of the Holy Sepulchre is a kind of metaphor for the state of a multifaceted Christianity in the 21st century.

Suggested Reading

Biddle et al., *The Church of the Holy Sepulchre*, chapter 1. The first chapter contains the history of the Holy Sepulchre, but be sure to glance through all the splendid photos.

Sacred Destinations, "Church of the Holy Sepulchre, Jerusalem," http:// www.sacred-destinations.com/israel/jerusalem-church-of-holy-sepulchre. A useful article plus good photographs are available on this site.

Questions to Consider

1. Why is pilgrimage such a powerful activity and metaphor for the Christian life, especially in relation to the Holy Sepulchre as expressed in the Stations of the Cross?

2. For a religion that believes in the incarnation of God in Jesus, why is being in the place where important events in Jesus's life too place, especially his place of burial and Resurrection, so compelling?

3. Looking forward to other churches that were destinations of pilgrims, how is pilgrimage both a practice of and a metaphor for the Christian life?

The aedicule, where according to Christian belief, Jesus was buried and, thus, the place of his Resurrection.

Modern entrance of the Holy Sepulchre.

13

Chapel of Golgotha; houses the place where the Cross was inserted into the top of the hill of Golgotha.

Place where Jesus's body was prepared for burial.

Ancient tomb discovered in the 20th century; probably similar to the original site over which the aedicule was built.

Chapel of the Holy Cross, where Helena is believed to have found the Cross.

Nave built in Crusader times; the largest open space in the Holy Sepulchre.

Modern dome mosaic of Christ.

Dome over the aedicule.

Hagia Sophia
Lecture 3

As mentioned in the last lecture, Constantine became the emperor of Rome in the 4th century. He decided to build a new capital—a Christian Rome—on the site of an ancient Greek city called Byzantium. He named his new city Constantinople, although we know it today, of course, as Istanbul. In 476, there ceased to be a Roman emperor in the west, and for the next 1,000 years, the only Roman emperor ruled from Constantinople, the largest Christian city in the world. The great cathedral of Constantinople is Hagia Sophia, which means "Holy Wisdom."

The building we see today is actually the third one built on the site because the second cathedral there was destroyed in a riot in the 520s. But the emperor Justinian immediately decided to rebuild Hagia Sophia—bigger and better than before. Construction on the new cathedral was begun in 532, and the church was dedicated just five years later. Hagia Sophia was the emperor's church and the seat of the patriarch (chief bishop) of Constantinople.

Of course, the church has experienced many changes in its 1,500-year history. In the 8th and 9th centuries, all the icons—that is, holy images, whether paintings, mosaics, or sculptures—were destroyed throughout the Byzantine Empire. Thus, virtually all of the original decoration of Hagia Sophia was destroyed. Then, in the 13th century, the Fourth Crusade captured Constantinople and made Hagia Sophia into a Roman Catholic church after looting it.

In 1261, a new Byzantine emperor from the east came to power, and the church once again became Greek Orthodox. In 1439, out of a kind of desperation stemming from the attack of the Turks on Constantinople, the Greeks agreed to a reunion with Rome, and Hagia Sophia was Catholic once again. But in 1453, the Ottoman Turks conquered Constantinople, and the church became a mosque. It served as a mosque until 1935, when Kemal Atatürk, the president of Turkey, declared it to be a museum.

Today, we see decorations of various periods of this history, including some marks of the Crusaders and much evidence that the church served as a mosque for about 500 years. In modern times, since Hagia Sophia has been a museum, a great deal of archaeological work has been done, and many beautiful works of art from its time as an Orthodox church have been uncovered.

Suggested Reading

Freely and Cakmak, *Byzantine Monuments of Istanbul*, chapter 6. This section deals with Hagia Sophia; pages 129–136 cover the elegant SS. Sergius and Bacchus.

Hagia Sophia, http://www.3dmekanlar.com/en/hagia-sophia.html. A virtual tour.

Questions to Consider

1. Thinking of the report to the Russian prince Vladimir, how is architecture an expression of the faith of Christians, both to those who worship there and to those who are not Christian?

2. What do you think of the conversion of a 900-year-old church into a mosque, keeping in mind that in Lecture 10, we will study a mosque in Córdoba that was turned into a cathedral after more than 400 years?

Exterior of Hagia Sophia.

Christ mosaic commissioned by Emperor Leo VI at the end of the 0ᵗʰ century.

Mosaic over the emperor's entrance.

Interior of Hagia Sophia.

Courtesy of Professor William R. Cook.

Recently discovered mosaic of the Madonna and Child, dating from the 9th century.

Carved pilaster.

Empress's gallery.

Mosaic of Christ, Mary, and John the Baptist; probably 13th century.

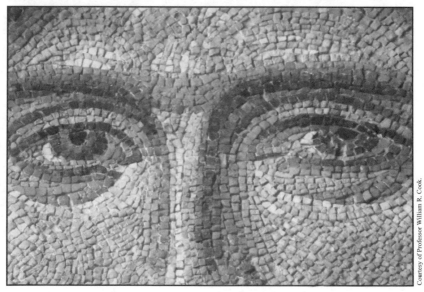

Detail of Christ's eyes.

The Cave Churches of Cappadocia
Lecture 4

Cappadocia is an area in central Turkey that has been Muslim for some time, but this area was also important in the beginnings of Christianity. St. Paul evangelized in Cappadocia, and several of the fathers of the church were from Cappadocia.

It is an unworldly-looking place, studded with geological formations called *fairy chimneys*. These spires are formed of deposits of different types of stone, which means that they erode at different rates, making odd shapes. Within these fairy chimneys and the hills of this region, many structures were carved out of stone, including small churches and monasteries. In fact, hundreds of these churches are still being discovered in Cappadocia. Some are quite small and plain, while others are large and elaborate, with beautiful painting. It's important to note that the churches here are not just rough-hewn but finished stone. Visitors get the impression that they are in a structure that has been built by human hands, rather than what is essentially a cave that has been hollowed out of rock.

The area of Cappadocia was raided by Arabs in the 7th century, although they didn't stay. The 9th to 11th centuries seem to have been great periods for the building and painting of these rock-hewn churches. After 1071, when the Byzantine Empire lost a major battle to the Seljuq Turks, the area came under Turkish domination and has been ever since, although at least for the first few centuries, Christianity was tolerated. Indeed, Christians lived in this region until the 1920s; after that, in a huge population swap, many Muslim Turks moved from Greece to the newly created state of Turkey following the collapse of the Ottoman Empire and many Christians moved to Greece.

There is virtually no documentation about any of the churches of Cappadocia. We don't know, for example, who they were dedicated to, who the painters were, or even what techniques were used to hollow out the fairy chimneys. Obviously, scholars and archaeologists have answered some of these questions, but Cappadocia remains, nevertheless, a place of mystery.

Kostof, *Caves of God.*

Rodley, *Cave Monasteries of Byzantine Cappadocia*, chapters 1–2. The first chapter introduces the reader to the churches of Cappadocia, and the second describes (alas, with only black-and-white photos) several of the most important monasteries of Cappadocia.

Turkish Heritage Travel, *Goreme Open-Air Museum*, http://www.goreme. com/goreme-open-air-museum.php. A broad look at the cave churches of Cappadocia.

Questions to Consider

1. How well do the almost 1,000-year-old frescoes of the cave churches of Cappadocia capture the meaning and essence of the biblical stories represented in them?

2. What are the implications for the communities of Christians who worshipped in the cave churches—laypeople, monks, and hermits— given that they are small and that there are so many separate sites of worship?

Dark-stone-topped fairy chimneys with "spires."

Selime Kilise.

Interior of Durmus Kadir (near the village of Göreme).

Detail of Kiss of Judas fresco, Church of the Holy Cross; probably 11th or 12th century.

Courtesy of Professor William R. Cook.

Göreme Open-Air Museum, containing about 10 surviving churches.

Courtesy of Professor William R. Cook.

Annunciation and Visitation, Buckle Church.

Dark Church dome.

Last Supper, Dark Church; note that *ichthys* (Greek: "fish") is an acronym for Jesus Christ, son of God, Savior.

Great Churches of Russia
Lecture 5

In this lecture, we find ourselves, for the first time, in a part of the world that was not part of the Roman Empire; therefore, the area that we call Russia was not Christian as early as Western Europe and the Mediterranean world. In fact, it was only at the end of the 10th century that the ruler of the Russians, Vladimir, decided to choose a new religion. He sent emissaries to various places where various religions were practiced—Judaism, Islam, different forms of Christianity—to determine what was the best religion to follow. He chose to follow the Christianity of Constantinople, partly because of the report he received from his emissary, describing Hagia Sophia:

> And we went into the Greek lands and we were led into a place where they served their God and we did not know where we were, on heaven or on earth. I do not know how to tell you about this. All we know is that God lives there with the priest, and their service is better than in any other country. We cannot forget that beauty since a person, if he eats something sweet, will not taste something bitter afterwards; so we cannot remain anymore in paganism.

Orthodoxy thus became the religion of Russia and, of course, is again today, after a number of interruptions— —whether the Mongols invading in the 13th century or the years of communism in the 20th. In many cases, the churches in Russia are similar to churches from the Byzantine Empire, but it's important to note that there are also Western influences in Russia.

In this lecture, we will travel through what is known as the Golden Ring, which is a series of cities to the north and east of Moscow that played a role in the development of the early Russian Orthodox Church. We'll begin in Moscow with the Cathedral of St. Basil. Although this is the most famous church in Russia, it is atypical of what the Russians achieved over centuries in building and decorating churches. There is really no precedent for this church, and there are no later churches that are modeled on St. Basil's.

From there, we will travel to Vladimir, which was the center of the church in Russia for a time, to see two cathedrals: the Assumption or Dormition Cathedral and St. Demetrius Cathedral. The first of these features frescoes by the famous Russian painter Andrei Rublev. We will then look at a number of other churches on the Golden Ring before returning to Moscow to explore some of the churches inside the Kremlin.

Suggested Reading

Brumfield, *A History of Russian Architecture*, chapters 3 and 5. These two chapters cover most of what is discussed in the lecture; the first focuses on the churches of the Golden Ring, and the second focuses on the churches of Moscow.

Moscow.Info, Inc., *Churches of the Kremlin*, http://www.moscow.info/ kremlin/churches/index.aspx. Here, you can click to examine each of the churches in Moscow's Kremlin.

Questions to Consider

1. What do we learn about the modern history of Russia when we look at what survived (and recognize what did not survive) during periods of invasion and the 70-plus years of the policies of the Soviet Union?

2. How does looking at the floor space and decorative schemes of Russian churches give us insight into the beliefs and practices of Orthodoxy as it was and is practiced in Russia?

St. Basil's Cathedral, Moscow.

Assumption or Dormition Cathedral, Vladimir.

Courtesy of Professor William R. Cook.

Exterior detail, St. Demetrius Cathedral, Vladimir; decoration dates from the 12th century.

© Sergey Orlov/iStock/Thinkstock.

Walled cathedral, Suzdal.

John the Baptist, Suzdal cathedral.

Main church, Kostroma.

Ascension Cathedral, Yaroslavl.

The Painted Churches of Romania
Lecture 6

In northeastern Romania is an area called Bukovina and, more broadly, Moldavia. This area is part of the Orthodox Christian world, but for several centuries, it was on the border between Christianity and Islam. In fact, we will see evidence of the frontier status of the walled monasteries in this region in the militant and tough Christianity depicted in their art. One of the peculiarities of the churches in this area is that they're not only frescoed on the inside but also on the outside. Obviously, a great of deal of damage has been done to the outside frescoes; nevertheless, the churches here are unique for the amount and quality of Christian art they display.

Most of the churches we will see in this lecture were built between the 13th and 17th centuries, and almost all the decorations date from the 16th and 17th centuries. Today, most of these churches, after the fall of communism in Romania in 1989, are once again occupied by those who have taken up a religious vocation, primarily nuns. Thus, when we visit these fairly remote monasteries in northeastern Romania, we are looking not just at monuments but also at holy places inhabited by the devout for most of their lives.

One interesting element we will see in Romania (and elsewhere) is the depiction of the Tree of Jesse. Jesse is the father of David, and the Bible prophecies that out of Jesse will come a tree; that tree is seen as being the ancestry of Jesus. We will also see many martyr stories on these frescoed churches, again, a reminder of their frontier status and the need for Christians to stand firm in their beliefs. Some of the frescoes show great processions of saints, bishops, patriarchs, and others—even the ancient philosopher Plato—who are journeying toward God. Inside the painted churches, we sometimes see calendars of saints—hundreds of stories depicted on the walls to show the faithful feast days throughout the year. None of the churches we will see in this lecture is very large, and few have elaborate doors or towers. But with frescoes covering both the outside and inside walls, the monasteries here are unlike anything we find anywhere else in the world.

Elo-Valente, *Bucovina*, sections on churches in this lecture. This book also allows readers to look at those churches that were not part of the lecture and, thus, gives an overview of the area's ecclesiastical structures.

Art of the Fresco, http://romania-monastery.info/. Interesting information about the art of fresco painting in Romania.

Questions to Consider

1. How do the Romanian monasteries both continue traditions, such as those we have seen in Russia, and adapt them to their time and place?

2. Thinking especially about the "calendars" painted in the entry rooms to these churches, how do you think the monks and nuns use the decorations of the churches, inside and outside, as guides to prayer and right teaching?

Walled monastery, Moldovita.

Angel sounding the Resurrection, Voronet Monastery, Romania.

Solomon in the Tree of Jesse, Voronet Monastery, Romania.

Creation of Eve, Voronet Monastery, Romania.

East end of painted church.

City of Constantinople besieged (7th century).

Dome with the Virgin Mary and Christ.

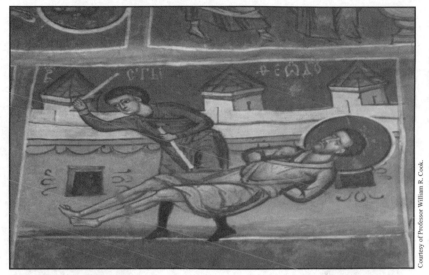

Scene of martyrdom.

Christ mocked.

Iconostasis.

The Churches of Armenia
Lecture 7

Armenia, a nation that bordered the Roman Empire, accepted Christianity in the year 301, making it the first political entity to adopt Christianity. A missionary from Syria whom we call St. Gregory the Illuminator was the one who brought Christianity to Armenia. In fact, in the year 2001, Pope John Paul II came to Yerevan, the modern capital of Armenia, and celebrated with the catholicos—the head of the Armenian apostolic church—1,700 years of Christianity in Armenia. And for most of that time, the Armenians have built and decorated extraordinary churches.

Unfortunately, many of the most extraordinary things that the Armenians built or, for that matter, wrote were destroyed in subsequent centuries because just about every nation within 1,000 miles has invaded Armenia at some time or another—Arabs, Mongolians, Turks, and of course, Russians. All of those groups brought destruction and, in some cases, a pause in the building and decorating of churches. Further, the shape of the modern nation of Armenia is different than it was in earlier times, when it was much larger—what is called Greater Armenia. Thus, at least one of the most important Armenian churches we'll see in this lecture is, in fact, in Turkey.

Among the notable qualities of the art of Armenian churches are its extraordinary detail and its decorative patterns. We will also explore the simplicity and delicacy of their architecture. In fact, it has been argued that the architects of Hagia Sophia in Istanbul were influenced by the traditional Armenian way of building churches. In some of the churches, we'll see a different kind of dome that may have been modeled on the tents used by Armenian nomads and shepherds. We'll also see reflections of Armenian history and even some pagan elements in the architecture of this region.

In modern times, the Armenians continue to build on their multi-century tradition of Christianity. When Pope John Paul II came to Yerevan, he participated in the dedication of a new cathedral there, one that has modern qualities yet unmistakably includes something of the Armenians' 1,700-year tradition of worshipping the Christian God, Christ, and the Holy Spirit.

Suggested Reading

Harada, *The Book of Ahtamar Reliefs*. There is not much material in English about the Armenian churches, but this book has excellent photos. Another way to get acquainted with the churches is with a good travel guide to Armenia, such as the Bradt guide.

Moscow.Info, Inc., *Churches of the Kremlin*, http://www.moscow.info/ kremlin/churches/index.aspx. A catalogue of the surviving medieval monasteries of Armenia.

Questions to Consider

1. How have the new cathedral in Yerevan and the baptistery in Echmiadzin developed and built on traditional Armenian Christian architecture, and how do they differ from it and, thus, challenge Armenian Christians to "modernize" their traditions?

2. What does the blend of pre-Christian, Western, Byzantine, and Muslim elements in Armenian churches tell us about Armenian history generally and the development of Armenian Christianity specifically?

Zvartnots Cathedral, near the modern capital of Yerevan; 7th century.

Church of St. Hripsime, Ejmiatsin; 7th century.

Story of Jonah, Church of the Holy Cross, Akdamar Island, Turkey; 9th–10th centuries.

Church with gavit, Noravank.

Exterior decoration, Trinity, Noravank.

Open dome, second church at Noravank.

Great church at Tatev dedicated to SS. Peter and Paul.

Monastery at Sanahin.

Unusual round church at Sanahin; 10th century.

Courtesy of Professor William R. Cook.

Interior of gavit, monastery of Haghpat.

The Churches of Georgia
Lecture 8

G eorgia is a little bit further away from the Roman Empire than Armenia, yet it became Christian just a few decades after Armenia did, in 337. The story of how the Georgians became Christian is particularly interesting, because the one who was responsible for converting the Georgians was a female, St. Nino.

Just as we saw in Armenia, Georgia has a long and interesting history of Christianity. Most of the churches we will see in this lecture are from the 13th century, but we will go back as far as the 11th century. There is nothing quite as old in Georgia as some of the Armenian churches, but as we'll see, more exterior decoration and more frescoes have survived in Georgia than Armenia. This may give us a better sense of what those churches would have looked like at the time they were completed.

We will begin our exploration of Christianity in Georgia with a visit to the city of Mtskheta, near the modern capital of Tbilisi, which is where St. Nino lived. The largest cathedral built in Georgia before the 20th century—as far as we know—is in Mtskheta, and again, because this was the frontier of Christianity, the cathedral is fortified. We will then travel into the countryside of Georgia to see a number of churches dating from the 11th to 13th centuries. The cathedral in Nikortsminda is perhaps the most interesting of these, with a dome supported by six pillars and beautiful frescoes throughout. We'll also visit the most famous church in Georgia, Gelati, which is a World Heritage site. This church retains the only surviving mosaic in Georgia, a depiction of the Madonna and Child and an angel. We'll close in Tbilisi itself, at Sameba Cathedral, built in modern times by a Georgian architect named Archil Mindiashvili. This cathedral begins with the basic Georgian model but adds layers to it. It is both traditional and modern, representing a new center of Christianity in a very old Christian country.

Suggested Reading

Soltes, ed., *National Treasures of Georgia*, part IV, chapters 1–4. Provides both context and description for further exploration of Georgia's monasteries. The Bradt guide to Georgia may also be useful.

Saints Peter and Paul Serbian Orthodox Church, "Monasteries and Churches in Georgia," http://atlantaserbs.com/learnmore/monasteries_and_towns/Gruzija.htm. On this website are descriptions and photographs of the most important Georgian monasteries.

Questions to Consider

1. What do you see as unique elements in Georgian architecture and, especially, in Georgian church decoration?

2. What are the advantages and disadvantages of the Georgians having so many of their most important churches, which were also centers of education, in such remote places?

Lecture 8: The Churches of Georgia

Mtshkheta Cathedral.

Nunnery of Santavro, Mtshkheta; by tradition, built over the place where St. Nino had her hut.

Timotesuban Monastery, with frescoes dating from the 12th and early 13th centuries.

Nikortsminda Cathedral.

Dome with six pillars, Nikortsminda Cathedral.

Christ prepared for burial.

Monastery of Gelati, near the city of Kutaisi.

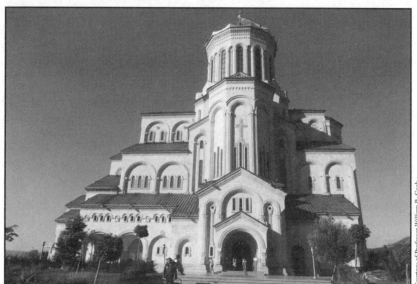

Sameba Cathedral, Tbilisi.

The Rock-Hewn Churches of Ethiopia
Lecture 9

In most of sub-Saharan Africa and Africa, Christianity is a rather recent phenomenon, brought by missionaries in the 18th century. But Ethiopia, although it is located in sub-Saharan Africa, has a somewhat different history. Because it has a major coastline, it was in communication and had relations with the Roman Empire. Thus, in the 4th century—the same century in which the Roman Empire, Armenia, and Georgia became Christian—the royal family of Ethiopia converted to Christianity. Probably in the 6th century, when missionaries from Syria came to Ethiopia, the region itself became Christian in a meaningful way.

However, the story of Ethiopia's relationship to and participation in Christianity is far older than simply its Christianization in the 4th or 6th century. In fact, Ethiopians have believed for many centuries that their kings are the direct descendants of King Solomon. According to Ethiopian tradition, the queen of Sheba, who famously visited King Solomon, was the queen of Ethiopia. She was made pregnant by Solomon and had a son named Menelik, who later went to Israel to find his father. While in Israel, Menelik took the Ark of the Covenant and brought it back to Ethiopia, where according to the Ethiopians, it remains in the city of Axum.

Interestingly, there is even a more direct connection between Christianity and Ethiopia in the New Testament: In the Acts of the Apostles, we're told that the first Gentile—that is, the first non-Jewish Christian—was an Ethiopian. This man read Hebrew scripture, believed in the Hebrew God, and came to one of the pilgrim festivals in Israel. Although we're not told what happened to this man, the Ethiopians believe that he returned to his homeland and founded a Christian community.

In addition, Ethiopians believe that when Jesus, Mary, and Joseph fled King Herod and came to Egypt, they also stayed in Ethiopia for a time. It's clear, then, that Ethiopia is a biblical country, with ties to both Hebrew and Christian scripture. It is a very old Christian culture, one that was, for many centuries, largely cut off from the majority of Christians around the Mediterranean and grew in distinctiveness over time.

Suggested Reading

Mercier and Lepage, *Lalibela*, chapter 2. The best book in English about the churches of Lalibela, with spectacular photographs. Not always compelling reading, but it is worth the effort.

Barnett, "Rock Churches of Lalibela," www.cnn.com/2013/06/27/travel/rock-churches-lalibela-ethiopia/. Watch the videos that are part of this CNN piece on Lalibela.

Questions to Consider

1. How do we see the interaction between the religious and the political in the creation of the churches of Lalibela?

2. From what you have seen and heard, to what extent is Ethiopian Christianity isolated from other Christian traditions and to what extent does it appear to be connected to Christianity elsewhere?

Savior of the World, Lalibela.

Church of Mary; probably the church of the emperor.

Courtesy of Professor William R. Cook.

Painted Madonna and Child, Church of Mary.

Church of Golgatha.

Church of Libanos, carved into the side of a hill.

Church of Mercurius.

Church of Emmanuel.

Cross on top of the Church of St. George.

The Mosque-Cathedral of Córdoba
Lecture 10

The Cathedral of Córdoba in Spain is quite an extraordinary place, and it's important to know a bit about its history as we examine the building itself. Spain was part of the Roman Empire, but in the 5th century, as the empire in the west was collapsing, Spain was conquered by a Germanic tribe called the Visigoths. Then, in 711, Muslims coming through North Africa conquered most of the Iberian Peninsula and established Muslim rule, which lasted in parts of Spain until 1492. The Cathedral of Córdoba represents all those layers of history.

On the spot where the cathedral now stands, there was, at one time, a pagan temple. In the 7th century, the Visigoths built a Christian church on top of the ruins of that temple. At the end of the 8th century, the Muslims built a mosque on top of the Visigothic church. Much of the mosque was finished by around 800, although it was added to until about the year 1000. In 1236, the Christians conquered Córdoba and reclaimed it for Christianity. The mosque was converted into a church again, beginning with the reign of King Ferdinand. But Ferdinand put the church literally in the middle of the mosque, creating an extraordinary and unique structure—part Muslim and part Christian.

The mosque was essentially a low building, with an almost-square enclosed courtyard. Most of it was occupied by rows of columns—856 in all. The entrance was once a minaret, but that has been transformed into the cathedral's bell tower. Inside the structure, visitors are astounded by the extraordinary number of arches, supported by a forest of columns. Because non-Muslims cannot enter a mosque, Córdoba is one of the few places in the world where Christians can appreciate the beauty of a medieval mosque. Also striking are the many juxtapositions of Western European Christian art and architecture with the elements of a Muslim holy building.

Today, an increasing Muslim population has immigrated to Spain, and members of this population have formally petitioned the Vatican to be allowed to worship in the space they created 1,200 years ago. Thus, there is an ongoing tension about the uses of this building in the 21st century. But Pope John Paul II visited Córdoba in the 1980s and noted that the building is also a place that can represent the joining in fraternity of people who profess the one God.

Suggested Reading

Menocal, *The Ornament of the World*, pp. 53–78. These pages present the Muslim city of Córdoba and its mosque.

Donadio, "Name Debate Echoes an Old Clash of Faiths," http://www.nytimes.com/2010/11/05/world/europe/05cordoba.html?pagewanted=all&_r=0. A *New York Times* article from a few years ago about controversies today regarding the cathedral and its Muslim origin.

Questions to Consider

1. Muslims in Spain have petitioned the Vatican for the right to pray in the Mezquita, which was, after all, a mosque for 400 years before the city's reconquest by Christians. Where do you stand on that request, and what do you think are the arguments for and against?

2. How should we think about the reuse of holy buildings and spaces, given that the location of the Mezquita had a Christian church (and perhaps before that a pagan temple) before the building of the mosque that was then transformed into a cathedral?

Cathedral of Córdoba.

© rognar/iStock/Thinkstock.

Interior of cathedral.

© master2/iStock/Thinkstock.

Courtesy of Professor William R. Cook.

Mosaics at the entrance to the *mihrab*.

© Maui01/iStock/Thinkstock.

Scalloped dome.

Madonna and Child under an 8th-century arch.

Altar in the cathedral.

Fan vault over the altar.

Choir stalls, with New Testament stories above and Old Testament stories below.

The Stave Churches of Norway
Lecture 11

A t the end of the 8th century and the beginning of the 9th century, Vikings sailed out of Norway and began to attack Christian Western Europe—England and France. Ultimately, they sailed into the Mediterranean. At first, these were raids, but later on, various Norse peoples began to move into the areas that they had been raiding, and when they did so, they became Christians. But those who stayed in Norway were not converted to Christianity until the 11th and 12th centuries; thus, it is primarily in the 12th century that we begin to find major churches in Norway made out of wood. These are known as *stave churches*.

At one time, there were about 1,000 stave churches in Norway; today, there are fewer than 30. By and large, these are in fairly remote parts of Norway, although one has been moved to a museum in Oslo. Some of the decoration of these churches looks similar to other elements of contemporary medieval art in Western Europe. But much of it is unique to the Norwegians because they, like all peoples when they adopt Christianity, took elements of their own culture, tradition, and preexisting religions and worked them into the Christian buildings they constructed.

Scholars disagree on the inspiration for the design of the stave churches. We know that there were wooden churches in England and that the Norse people raided in England. Some scholars believe that the Norwegians copied or at least borrowed from English wooden churches. There are also those who say that the wooden churches are Norwegians' attempt to replicate Christian basilicas in wood and in their own tradition. Still others argue that the stave churches are probably more of an indigenous style and not particularly deeply influenced by outsiders at all.

Of course, many of these wooden churches were burned or otherwise destroyed. It's also true that in the 16th century, Norway became Lutheran; thereafter, several of these churches were fairly radically transformed to fit the new form of Christianity that was being practiced in Norway. Many things that would have been associated with Catholicism were probably destroyed at that time. Given that history, it's somewhat of a miracle that even some of these churches have survived and are carefully preserved into the 21st century.

Suggested Reading

Anker and Havran, *The Norwegian Stave Churches*. This brief and well-illustrated book allows a look at all of the surviving medieval wood churches of Norway.

Innovation Norway, *Visitnorway.com*, "Stave Churches," http://www.visitnorway.com/us/About-Norway/History/Stave-churches/. A list, with photos, of the surviving stave churches in Norway.

Questions to Consider

1. How might these churches look today if the Protestant Reformation had not occurred in Norway?

2. From the art that remains in these churches, how can we imagine that medieval Norwegian Christians understood their faith?

Church of Borgund.

Church of Lom, with later transept and stone foundation.

Church of Lom interior.

Church of Urnes; 12th century.

Church of Hedal, 13th century.

Exterior decoration, Hedal.

Interior decoration, Torpo.

77

Colored sculpture, Hopperstad.

The Pilgrimage Church of Sainte-Foy
Lecture 12

Two of the most important pilgrimage sites for Western Europeans living in the Middle Ages were Jerusalem and the Santiago de Compostela in Spain, said to house the body of the earliest martyred apostle, James. The Santiago de Compostela is a Romanesque church in the northwestern corner of Spain, an area that was not under Muslim control. The church we'll explore in this lecture, however, is in a fairly remote part of south-central France in a small village called Conques.

This church was an important stop on one particular pilgrimage route that led to Santiago. The route started in the French city of Le Puy, a gathering place for pilgrims who were coming from further east—from Germany and beyond. One of the first major stops on this route on the way to Santiago de Compostela was Conques. The church there housed the relics of St. Faith, or Sainte Foy, martyred as a 12-year-old girl. Sainte Foy was invoked against poor eyesight and blindness and to free men who had been imprisoned by Muslims in the Crusades. Although the church at Conques was not the final destination of many pilgrimages, a stop there would have given pilgrims the benefit of visiting other relics and shrines of saints before reaching the ultimate goal of their pilgrimage.

Sainte-Foy is, in essence, a basilica. However, as we've already seen in one of the remodeled churches in Norway—the Church of Lom in the last lecture—basilicas were sometimes expanded by adding a *transept*—essentially the crossbar of a cross. Thus, when visitors enter the church, they are entering the Cross of Christ. As they walk through, they're approaching the place where the head of Christ would be, which is also where the Eucharist would be celebrated. Although most churches of this time were, in fact, this modified form of basilica, we should recognize that it's a specifically Christian modification of the ancient basilical plan.

When they arrived in Conques, pilgrims encountered a magnificent church, again, built in the Romanesque style. This church is known for its tympanum, depicting the Last Judgment. For the Benedictine monks who lived at Sainte-Foy, the tympanum would have served as a constant reminder of the coming judgment. The pilgrims would have had the experience of praying to Sainte Foy, going to mass in the church, and perhaps even sleeping there. When they walked away, the tympanum might prompt them to contemplate the dangers of the journey to Santiago and the rewards they hoped to obtain from completing that journey.

Suggested Reading

Harmel, "The Tympanum of Conques in Detail." This pamphlet provides great detailed analysis of the tympanum of Conques.

Office de Tourisme, Conques, "The Tympanum of the Last Judgment," http://www.tourisme-conques.fr/en/histoire-patrimoine/eglise-abbatiale/tympan-jugement-dernier.php. This site provides a detailed description and photos of the tympanum.

Questions to Consider

1. Given the building, the cult statue, and the tympanum, how can we imagine the response to this site of pilgrims on their way to Santiago?

2. How does the tympanum contain a "dialogue" between the teachings and understandings of the Catholic Church generally and the community of monks and their visitors, the pilgrims, in Conques? How does it express (and resolve) the tension between universal and particular?

Church of Sainte-Foy.

Reliquary of Sainte Foy.

Gallery detail.

Crossing tower.

Painted angel sculpture.

Courtesy of Professor William R. Cook.

Capital with Sainte Foy.

© Zoonar/N.Sorokin/Zoonar/Thinkstock.

Tympanum, Last Judgment.

Entrances to heaven and hell, tympanum.

Sainte Foy and the hand of God, tympanum.

The Cathedral of Monreale
Lecture 13

I n the ancient and medieval world, Sicily was an extraordinarily cosmopolitan place. Even today, visitors to Sicily can see Greek and Roman ruins, along with buildings built by Byzantines, Muslims, French, Spanish, and others. The Cathedral of Monreale is in a village above the city of Palermo in Sicily and is a reflection of that cosmopolitanism. In this cathedral, built in the late 12th century, we will see Muslim, Byzantine, Frankish, Italian, and even Jewish influences and inspiration.

Why did the village of Monreale become the seat of a great cathedral? It's probably the case that the late-12th-century king William II, a Norman, decided to curb the power of the archbishop of Palermo by establishing another archbishop close by. Interestingly, this cathedral also has a monastery attached to it, an unusual feature in Italy. The cloister itself is so beautiful that even if the cathedral did not exist, it would still attract visitors. Because Muslims controlled most of the island of Sicily for several centuries, we'll see Islamic influences here in the prominence of a wash basin, rows of double columns, and inlaid mosaics. The interlocking archways on the outside of the east end of the cathedral are also reminiscent of Islamic workmanship.

Of course, the most stunning feature of Monreale is its mosaics—pictures of biblical stories and events, saints' lives, and so on, as well as decorative work that appears around windows, on walls, on marble steps, and more. In fact, it's been calculated that this cathedral has four acres of mosaics on the walls. The building itself is a basilica with a transept—a Western style of building—but much of the work inside seems to have been done by Muslims or those operating in a tradition of Muslim craftsmanship. In this lecture, we'll examine the incredible intricacy, subtlety, and detail of some of this mosaic work, focusing in particular on the image of Christ Pantokrator ("Great Judge"), a mosaic more than 40 feet tall to which visitors are drawn from the moment they enter the cathedral.

Sciortino, *The Cathedral of Monreale*. The photos are great, and the first few chapters give a detailed description of the decorations.

Planetware, "Monreale Cathedral," http://www.planetware.com/monreale/monreale-cathedral-i-si-monct.htm. This website contains a good diagram of the church and cloister plus a map of all the mosaics in the cathedral.

Questions to Consider

1. How might Christians reconcile all of the gold and elegance of Monreale Cathedral with the simplicity and poverty of Christ and the early church?

2. How might all of the stories on the walls of Monreale reinforce the liturgical celebrations in the cathedral, and how does the Pantokrator help Christians to remember God as a God of justice?

Cloister of Monreale.

Carved capitals, Last Judgment.

Exterior detail, showing Muslim influence.

Reused Roman capital.

Interior of Monreale.

Courtesy of Professor William R. Cook.

Christ Pantokrator, "Christ the Judge."

Courtesy of Professor William R. Cook.

St. Thomas of Becket.

Baptism of Jesus.

Courtesy of Professor William R. Cook.

91

Chartres Cathedral
Lecture 14

When most people think of a large church, they probably imagine a Gothic church. This is partly because of the success of the Gothic style; it's been argued that more stone was quarried in Europe in the 13th century than any other century, primarily to build these great Gothic cathedrals. We also think of Gothic churches because there was a great revival of Gothic in the 19th century, giving us St. Patrick's Cathedral in New York and the National Cathedral in Washington, DC. Of all these cathedrals, however, most scholars would probably agree that the most famous is the Cathedral of Chartres.

Chartres Cathedral was an important pilgrimage site in the Middle Ages because it claimed to have the cloak the Virgin Mary was wearing when she gave birth to Jesus. In addition, the town of Chartres was arguably one of the most important intellectual centers in Europe, producing some of the great scholars of the 12th century. In fact, one window inside the cathedral shows us a famous image from one of these scholars, Bernard of Chartres: that the great minds of the day are all like dwarfs, sitting on the shoulders of giants. The window depicts the evangelists Matthew, Mark, Luke, and John sitting on the shoulders of the prophets Daniel, Ezekiel, Isaiah, and Jeremiah. The theological message here is that the prophets could see only dimly, but the evangelists can see face to face.

Chartres is a rather elaborate basilica, with a great deal of sculpture on the porches of the transept. It's almost miraculous that Chartres' sculptures and stained-glass windows have survived from the 12th and 13th centuries. Consider that the cathedral survived the Wars of Religion in France in the 16th century, the remodeling of many cathedrals during the Enlightenment in the 18th century, the French Revolution at the end of the 18th century, and World War II, when every piece of stained glass was removed and packed away to protect it from the Nazis.

We should also note that the cathedral burned down in 1194, and the people of Chartres believed that their relic of the Virgin had been destroyed. The discovery that the relic was safe inspired the movement to construct an even greater shrine to the Virgin, beginning in 1294.

Suggested Reading

Miller, *Chartres Cathedral* and *Chartres Cathedral: Medieval Masterpieces in Stained Glass and Sculpture*. Miller's combination of knowledge of and passionate love for Chartres Cathedral is unbeatable.

Chartres Cathedral, http://www.medievalart.org.uk/chartres/Chartres_default.htm. On this site, you can look at both a photograph and a panel-by-panel description of each window at Chartres.

Questions to Consider

1. Chartres Cathedral was built as a proper shrine for the Virgin Mary after the fire of 1194. If that was the goal of the builders, were they successful and in what ways?

2. If polled, scholars of cathedrals would probably give Chartres Cathedral the highest rank in the world. Why might they do that? From what you have seen in this course and in your travels and study, do you agree with that evaluation of Chartres?

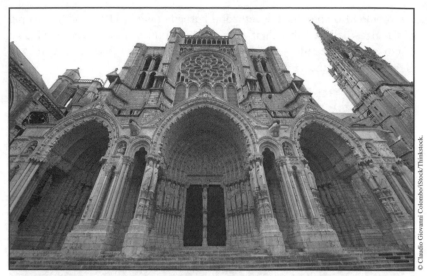

Chartres façade.

Jamb statues, presumed to be Old Testament kings and queens.

Lecture 14: Chartres Cathedral

Nativity tympanum.

Detail of Nativity, Incarnation window; 12th century.

Courtesy of Professor William R. Cook.

John the Baptist, north porch portal sculpture.

Shoemakers' window.

Zodiac window.

Winchester Cathedral
Lecture 15

If we're going to look at only one cathedral or church in England, Winchester is not the most obvious choice. The largest cathedral in England, for example, is a neo-Gothic one in the city of Liverpool. Canterbury Cathedral might be another good choice because it is the seat of the primate of England in the Church of England, the archbishop of Canterbury. York Cathedral is another large and beautiful cathedral and the seat of the only other archbishop in England, the archbishop of York. Salisbury Cathedral and Lincoln Cathedral are also famous sites in England. But Winchester Cathedral is interesting because it contains a variety of styles. It is largely a Gothic cathedral, but it has a Romanesque transept. And the different styles within the Gothic style are all represented in Winchester. This cathedral is truly a handbook of later medieval architecture and a wonderful blending of different phases of the development of style in England and Europe.

In addition, Winchester was the shrine of St. Swithin and an important pilgrimage site. St. Swithin was an early medieval bishop of Winchester, but he was known for his miracle working after he died. Although the shrine of St. Swithin was destroyed, Winchester remains a pilgrimage church—a dimension that is often forgotten about this building.

Even more than those things, however, Winchester Cathedral has extraordinary medieval wood carving and some interesting elements of medieval fresco, both of which are quite rare in England. It has a piece of floor of the original tile, which is still rarer. And it has one of the greatest holy books in all the world—a copy of the Bible done in the 12th century, the Winchester Bible. Last but not least, Winchester Cathedral has a series of unique tombs—important not just for their occupants but for their design and decoration.

Suggested Reading

Donovan, *The Winchester Bible*. Take the opportunity to learn about one of the most beautiful of all medieval manuscripts.

Winchester Cathedral. A thorough overview of both the architecture and the decoration.

Winchester Cathedral, http://winchester-cathedral.org.uk/gallery/?album =1&gallery=11. Good links to various features of Winchester Cathedral, including the Winchester Bible.

Questions to Consider

1. A cathedral that also was a monastery is peculiarly English. What are the needs of each, and how did Winchester Cathedral play the two quite different roles? Does this building work for both "audiences"?

2. When the Puritans, who were iconoclasts, ruled in England in the 17th century, what *should* they have done with regard to the art in the cathedral, which they considered illicit and un-Christian?

Norman (Romanesque) arch.

Courtesy of Professor William R. Cook.

Winchester Cathedral.

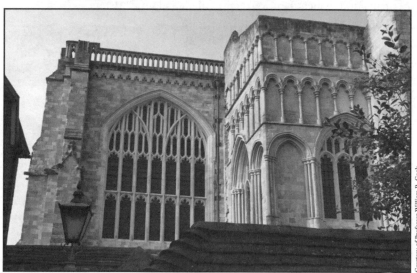

Lady chapel.

Fan vaulting.

Crossing tower.

Detail of fresco inside the Holy Sepulchre.

Stone wall.

Chantry of Henry Beaufort, bishop of Winchester.

The Cathedral of Siena
Lecture 16

S iena was an independent nation—a city-state—until 1555, when it was conquered by Florence and became part of the Grand Duchy of Tuscany. There are many reasons for us to look at Siena's cathedral—some of them artistic and some of them relating to our theme that churches are about people and places, not just architectural or painting styles or theologies. As we'll see, the Cathedral of Siena is a civic symbol as much as it is a religious edifice.

The cathedral was finished enough that masses were held there in 1215. But in 1296, the Florentines decided to rebuild the Cathedral of Florence, making it much larger and grander than Siena's cathedral. In response, the Sienese decided to make their structure grander than Florence's. But Siena had a problem in that its cathedral was on top of a hill; the Sienese couldn't just build on to either the front or the back of it. They hit on the idea of rotating the axis of the cathedral 90 degrees, making one arm of the transept into part of the nave and building a new nave. It would have been the largest cathedral in the world, but with the coming of the Black Death, Siena lost more than half of its population, and it was no longer possible to build something on such a grand scale.

As it stands today, the cathedral has a great bell tower and a glorious façade. It is a kind of hybrid Gothic cathedral, with elements from the Renaissance and the Baroque periods. In fact, we will find decorations here from almost every century, including the 20th. The cathedral also has a great deal of wonderful art, including sculpture by Michelangelo, Bernini, and Donatello and the great altarpiece the *Maestà* by Duccio. Note that none of these artists is a Sienese. From the beginning, the Sienese brought in artists from other places—even from their rivals, such as Florence—to decorate their great building to the glory of God and to the glory of Siena.

Suggested Reading

Carli, *Siena Cathedral and the Cathedral Museum*. This short book is a masterful overview of the Cathedral of Siena.

Olga's Gallery, "Duccio di Buoninsegna," http://www.abcgallery.com/D/duccio/maesta.html. Here, you can see each individual part of Duccio's *Maestà*, the altarpiece of the high altar of the medieval cathedral of Siena.

Questions to Consider

1. Given the principle of separation of church and state practiced in the United States, how do you regard the Cathedral of Siena, which was unabashedly both a religious and a civic building?

2. How do you respond to a church where you are surrounded (floor, pulpit, windows, painted altarpiece) by art? Is all of this art an education and aid to worship or a distraction?

Courtesy of Professor William R. Cook.

Cathedral of Siena.

Statue of Aristotle by Giovanni Pisano.

St. Michael, the Archangel.

Altarpiece of 1261, celebrating the victory of the Sienese over the Florentines at the Battle of Montaperti.

Siena and other cities represented on the floor.

Piccolomini library, frescoed by Pinturicchio; 15th–16th century.

Nicola Pisano pulpit; 1260s.

Lecture 16: The Cathedral of Siena

Statue of Mary Magdalene by Bernini.

St. Peter's Basilica
Lecture 17

St. Peter's in Rome is one of the most iconic buildings in the world—famous for its architecture and for Michelangelo's dome and *Pietà*. And, of course, more than any other church, we see it in the news because it's so intimately associated with the papacy—the institution that governs or leads more than 1 billion Catholics.

Although this building is relatively new, dating from the 16th and 17th centuries, the site is actually much older than that, which is true of almost everywhere in Rome. In ancient times, there was a circus here, a racetrack for horses. According to a very old and probably reliable tradition, in the mid-60s, St. Peter was crucified upside down in that circus.

In the 4th century, Constantine commissioned a basilica to be built over the place where Peter was buried, on a street with a cemetery adjacent to the circus. Only in the 20th century was the ancient Roman circus, the street next it, and the cemetery rediscovered, because it had been covered by various layers. Many important events took place in the original building, including the crowning of Charlemagne as Roman emperor on Christmas Day in the year 800. Less than half a century later, St. Peter's was attacked and badly damaged by a raid of Arabs who had crossed the Mediterranean and sailed up the Tiber. We have almost no decorations left from the old St. Peter's. One image in the Piccolomini chapel that we saw in the last lecture shows the original church as a simple basilica with a wooden roof and a mosaic above the altar.

For most of the 14th century and part of the 15th century, the popes lived in Avignon, not Rome. In their absence, St. Peter's essentially crumbled. At the beginning of the 16th century, Pope Julius II made the decision to tear down the original St. Peter's—then more 1,000 years old—and erect a new cathedral. An architect from Milan named Bramante was the first architect of the new St. Peter's, and he designed a Greek cross church. Successors to Bramante, including Michelangelo, changed his plans. The church we have today still has a huge central dome, but it also has an extraordinarily long nave. Among other things that make St. Peter's famous is the fact that it's the largest church in the world. And, of course, visiting St. Peter's is one of the most unforgettable experiences in all of Christendom.

Suggested Reading

Wallace, *Michelangelo*, chapter 11. Here is the masterful art historian's examination of Michelangelo's career at the time of his work on St. Peter's. Listen also to Lecture 31 in Wallace's offering from The Great Courses, *The Genius of Michelangelo*.

Saintpetersbasilica.org, http:// www.saintpetersbasilica.org/. This is perhaps the best website for any of the churches we are studying. You can find everything here—diagrams, art, and all sorts of interesting information.

Questions to Consider

1. St. Peter's is clearly a triumphalist church for Roman Catholicism. Should there be churches that are designed to promote a particular form of Christianity and implicitly denounce other forms of Christianity?

2. Although St. Peter's obviously displays the power and doctrinal claims of the Roman Church, does it also express the essence of Catholic and Christianity spirituality?

St. Peter's Square.

Michelangelo's dome.

Clock above the entrance.

Interior of basilica.

Courtesy of Professor William R. Cook.

Michelangelo's *Pietà*.

Courtesy of Professor William R. Cook.

Sculpture over arches.

Mosaic of Peter striking people dead.

Statue of Gregory XV.

The Wieskirche in Bavaria
Lecture 18

In this lecture, we will travel to Bavaria, the southern and most Catholic part of Germany, to see a pilgrimage church built in the 18th century in the style known as *rococo*. This style is a development out of baroque, which is itself a development out of the Renaissance style.

As you may know, Catholics in many parts of Europe participated in processions. Indeed, still today, in Spain, the news covers great parades of people carrying crosses and other symbols of the events of Holy Week. Such processions are also known in Italy and Germany. In 1738, a statue that showed Christ being beaten, primarily the work of an artist named Dominikus Zimmerman, was rejected from a procession for reasons of taste. But later on, a couple who was venerating the statue claimed that it wept. As a result, the statue became an important cult object, and soon, there was a demand to build a church to house it. Thus, in 1754, a church called the Wieskirche was consecrated in Bavaria.

Everything about the Wieskirche strikes us as different from other churches we've seen. It is oval in shape, and because it was decorated all at one time, it has a consistency of theme that we don't often see elsewhere. As mentioned, the interior decoration is in the rococo style, which was designed to be playful, entertaining, and pleasing to the eye. It was a style created for secular spaces, such as palaces or civic buildings, rather than churches. In some ways, then, it seems as if this style would need to be transformed to become the style of a holy place. The dark themes of the Wieskirche—penance and sin—seem to be even more challenging to reconcile with the joyful rococo style. But as we will see, the pilgrims who come here can learn and be inspired by the art around them. In this church, they can see the door of heaven, which is closed, but they know how they need to live to open that door.

Suggested Reading

Kirchmeir and Hasenmuller, *The Wies*. This small book contains a good overview of the Wieskirche and a careful look at all the details of its decoration.

Wieskirche, http://www.wieskirche.de/eframset.htm. Not a particularly good website, but it contains some history and decent photos.

Questions to Consider

1. Given that we usually think of rococo as a largely secular style, how have the designers and decorators of the Wieskirche attempted to transform it into a sacred style? Were they successful?

2. Does a style of art that so emphasizes movement aid or detract from pilgrims pondering the eternal?

Wieskirche.

Lecture 18: The Wieskirche in Bavaria

Courtesy of Professor William R. Cook.

Rococo interior.

St. Mark, stucco statue.

Angels with instruments of Christ's Passion.

Christ performing an exorcism.

Courtesy of Professor William R. Cook.

Throne of God.

Courtesy of Professor William R. Cook.

Gate to heaven.

Angel, part fresco and part statue.

La Compañía and Las Lajas Sanctuary
Lecture 19

As we all know, Christianity didn't exist in the Americas until the arrival of Columbus and the Spaniards in 1492. From the very earliest times, members of religious orders—in particular, Franciscans and Dominicans—accompanied those early voyages to America, built the first Christian buildings, and made the first Christian converts. For example, the oldest cathedral in the Americas is in the city of Santo Domingo in the Dominican Republic, founded by the Dominicans. In this lecture, we will look first at a church of the Society of Jesus—the Jesuits—in Quito, Ecuador. We will then turn to a shrine to the Virgin Mary in the southern part of Colombia.

Quito is one of the best preserved colonial cities of the Americas. In 1586, a new order, the Society of Jesus, arrived in Quito. Just a few years later, the members of this order began to build what's simply called the Church of a Society of Jesus, or La Compañía. In the 1630s, Marcos Guerra, an Italian Jesuit, came to Quito and added a bit of Italian influence to the largely Spanish baroque style that was being constructed for La Compañía. Thus, the style of the church is primarily European, but much of the execution of the decoration was done by local artists—sculptors, goldsmiths, and so on—from Ecuador.

The other church we'll visit in this lecture is Las Lajas in southern Colombia, an important site for pilgrimage to the Virgin Mary. In 1764, in a gorge in this region, a deaf girl found a painting of the Virgin Mary, Christ, St. Francis, and St. Dominic in a cave. Almost immediately, the cave became a place of pilgrimage, and various kinds of structures were built to accommodate pilgrims. But in the early 20th century, it was decided to build a larger and more proper shrine to the Virgin Mary, one that would encompass the cave where the painting had been found. The problem was that the cave is 100 meters from the bottom of the gorge.

The structure that was created is Our Lady of Las Lajas, which is built up from the bottom of the gorge. Visitors walk across a bridge to the church, jutting out of the side of a mountain; inside is the cave with the painting in it, making Las Lajas one of the most dramatic Marian shrines of them all. It's important to note, too, that this shrine remains part of a living tradition of pilgrimage. Many people come to pray for miracles and leave plaques thanking the Virgin for her intersession. To view these plaques covering the hills of the gorge that surrounds the church is a moving and intimate experience.

Suggested Reading

There is really no good material in English about either La Compañía or Las Lajas. The closest thing to reading material is in guidebooks to Quito and Colombia, respectively.

Guardian Angel, "Las Lajas Cathedral," http://www.guardianangel.in/ga/192-GuardianStory-Las-Lajas-Cathedral.html. Provides some historical information about Las Lajas plus several good photographs.

"Tour Virtual: La Compañía de Jesús," http://www.qpqweb.com/index.php?option=com_content&view=article&id=55&Itemid=68. Quite a fine virtual tour, although it takes a bit of figuring out because the instructions are in Spanish.

Questions to Consider

1. How might La Compañía have been effective in attracting the native population to Christianity and educating them in its basic teachings?

2. In both La Compañía and Las Lajas, how are European forms used outside Europe to promote the church and inspire the faithful?

Façade of La Compañía; 18th century.

Interior of La Compañía.

Sacred Heart of Jesus.

Courtesy of Professor William R. Cook.

Joseph flees Potiphar's wife.

Courtesy of Professor William R. Cook.

Dome of La Compañía

St. Ignatius Loyola, founder of the Jesuits.

Courtesy of Professor William R. Cook.

Shrine of Las Lajas.

Guadalupe and the Cathedral of Mexico City
Lecture 20

In December of 1531, a peasant named Juan Diego had a series of visions of the Virgin Mary in a place near Mexico City. In the last of those visions, although it was winter, many flowers grew around the place where the Virgin had appeared. Juan Diego gathered the flowers into his cloak and went off to show them to the Franciscan bishop of Mexico as a way of demonstrating the validity of his claims that he had seen the Virgin. When he unfolded the cloak, the flowers fell out, but he also discovered, as did the bishop, that the image of Our Lady of Guadalupe was imprinted on the cloak. This was the beginning of the great shrine of Our Lady of Guadalupe in Mexico. Today, more than 20 million people visit the shrine every year, making it one of the most important places in Christendom.

The complex at Guadalupe includes the old baroque basilica, a concrete basilica built in the 20th century to accommodate more people, a chapel on the hill where Juan Diego experienced the last of his apparitions, and other buildings. The decorations at Guadalupe encompass a kind of conversation among three potentially different entities: Spaniards, Christians, and indigenous people of the New World.

The other site we'll explore in this lecture is the Metropolitan Cathedral, or the Cathedral of Mexico City. Less than 30 years after Columbus first sailed to the New World, Hernán Cortéz destroyed the Aztec nation and its capital city and, shortly thereafter, began the construction of this cathedral. The Metropolitan Cathedral is dedicated to the Assumption of the Virgin Mary and is built on the site of the Templo Mayor ("Main Temple") of the Aztecs. The cathedral has been rebuilt more than once, and the building today dates primarily from the 17th, 18th, and 19th centuries. It stands in the historical part—the cultural heart—of Mexico City.

Both the Metropolitan Cathedral and the complex of Our Lady of Guadalupe are eloquent statements of both beautiful art and the extraordinary joining of many elements—saints, beliefs, and traditions—in the New World.

Johnston, *The Wonder of Guadalupe*, chapters 2–4. These chapters narrate the events involving the apparition of the Virgin to Juan Diego.

The Basilica of Guadalupe, http://www.sancta.org/basilica.html. With its links and a brief history, this website helps to introduce people to the shrine of Our Lady of Guadalupe.

Mexico City Metropolitan Cathedral, http://www.infosources.org/what_is/ Mexico_City_Metropolitan_Cathedral.html. Includes the history of the cathedral and descriptions of various elements.

Questions to Consider

1. As archaeologists discover pre-Christian remains under the Cathedral of Mexico City, what lessons should be learned, and what respect do those remains deserve?

2. How did the vision of Juan Diego and the relic and shrine of Our Lady of Guadalupe help to establish Christianity, and how do they continue to invigorate it?

Statue of Juan Diego.

Pocito chapel.

Old and new Basilica de Guadalupe

Peter and Paul on the entrance to the hill chapel.

Cathedral of Mexico City.

Assumption of the Virgin.

Façade of Metropolitan Cathedral parish church.

© King Ho Yim/iStock/Thinkstock.

Altar of Forgiveness.

Courtesy of Professor William R. Cook.

Four Great American Churches
Lecture 21

The first Christian service performed in what is now the 50 states probably took place in the 1560s in Saint Augustine, Florida. Of course, that would have been a Catholic mass in Latin. If we look more broadly at the coming of Christianity into the 50 states, we can note two early trends: the Spanish Catholic missionaries coming into what is now largely part of the American Southwest and the pilgrims and other Protestants coming to New England, along with Anglicans coming to Virginia, at the beginning of the 17th century. The latter trend gives us what most of us probably picture when we think of a typical American church: something like the First Church of Guilford in Connecticut, a 19th-century building sitting on a town square. In this lecture, we'll look at the First Church of Guilford and three other very different American churches.

Probably the most iconic church in the United States is the Old North Church in Boston. It was modeled on a late-17th-century church in London, built by Sir Christopher Wren. Of course, the tower of the Old North Church is what makes it famous to most Americans, owing to the great poem by Henry Wadsworth Longfellow, "Paul Revere's Ride." In commemoration of that poem, on April 18, 1976, President Gerald Ford hung a lantern inside the Old North Church, meant to be a beacon for America in its third century.

A different kind of building that housed a very different kind of Christian community is the Quaker meetinghouse in Pawling, New York, a small village just on the border with Connecticut. Built around 1764 and used as a hospital by George Washington's troops during the American Revolution, this structure is particularly well preserved and is now a museum. What qualifies this simple meetinghouse as a "great church"? As we've said, one of the things that makes a church great is that the building expresses the beliefs and values of its community. In this church, we see evidence of the equality and austerity practiced by the Quakers. The simplicity of this meetinghouse seems to speak eloquently of who the Quakers are and harks back to the early followers of Jesus, capturing something of Christian worship that we have not seen much celebrated in the other churches we've explored.

Finally in this lecture, we'll look at the National Cathedral in Washington, DC. Although it is an Episcopal cathedral, it welcomes people of all denominations, as well as non-Christians. This building was begun in 1907 and designed in the English style of Gothic architecture. Many important events in American history have taken place here. Martin Luther King Jr. gave his last Sunday sermon in the National Cathedral, and the funeral of President Ronald Reagan was held here. It is also the final resting place of President Woodrow Wilson. The cathedral is wonderfully decorated with stained-glass windows depicting both biblical scenes and modern events and people, including George Washington Carver, Robert E. Lee, Dr. Albert Schweitzer, and others. Perhaps the most dramatic of these windows is one dedicated to space—to the exploration of God's creation beyond the earth.

Suggested Reading

Dawson and Vochinsky, *Washington National Cathedral Guidebook.* It is good to browse through this book to get a sense of the totality of the decoration, including the stained glass, of the National Cathedral.

Wikimedia Commons, "Stained Glass Windows of the Washington National Cathedral." http://commons.wikimedia.org/wiki/Category:Stained_glass_windows_of_the_Washington_National_Cathedral. Not highly recommended, but this website allows visitors to examine and interpret many of the stained-glass windows in the National Cathedral.

Questions to Consider

1. Compare the way the National Cathedral in Washington, DC, and the Cathedral of Siena are both civic and religious buildings. Do they serve those dual functions in the same way, given the difference between medieval Siena and modern Washington?

2. How does the plurality of forms of Christianity and Christian buildings in the United States help us understand both the diversity and the unity of the United States in the past and the present?

Old North Church, Boston.

© Keith Levit Photography/Thinkstock.

Old North Church organ.

Courtesy of Professor William R. Cook.

First Church of Guilford, Connecticut.

Courtesy of Professor William R. Cook.

Guilford interior.

Quaker meetinghouse, Pawling, New York.

National Cathedral, Washington, DC.

Creation of Adam and Eve.

143

Altar and reredos.

La Sagrada Família
Lecture 22

In this lecture and the next two, we will look at three 20th-century buildings that, at least on the surface, don't look much like the earlier buildings we've seen. We will see ways in which Christianity and modern imagination and architecture meet in three very different places: in Barcelona, Iceland, and Korea.

Modern Barcelona is a city of 1.5 million people, and in a city of that size, we might expect skyscrapers to dominate the skyline. But that's not the case in Barcelona. What dominates is a church that's still under construction: La Sagrada Família, the Holy Family. It's an extraordinary building, begun at the end of the 19th century; it may be completed around the year 2050. The church was founded by a group called the Devotees of Saint Joseph; thus, St. Joseph and the Holy Family are central to the art of this church.

La Sagrada Família was built in a place where the old section of Barcelona was expanding and toward some villages that would become part of greater Barcelona in the 20th century. Thus, it straddles the old and new, and this geographical location is also, in some ways, its spiritual location. On the one hand, La Sagrada Família is a Gothic church, but at the same time, it is a modern structure quite unlike anything else in the world.

The original architect of La Sagrada Família was dismissed after a short time, and the architect Antoni Gaudí was given the job of working on this building, which he did for 43 years. In fact, Gaudí spent the last 12 years of his life exclusively on La Sagrada Família, although the church remained unfinished at the time of his death in 1926 and, in fact, is unfinished today. Toward the end of the 20th century, part of the structure was executed by an artist named Josep Maria Subirachs, who style was very different from Gaudí's. Some say that the work of Subirachs fits the spirit of Gaudí perfectly, while others see it as a kind of betrayal.

La Sagrada Família is a cruciform basilica. Thus, however strange and different this church may look, it is not a complete break with traditional Christian churches, as it's often depicted. It also represents continuity between the old and the new—and it is that combination that makes La Sagrada Família so fascinating. If we look at the church from one angle, it's very traditional. If we look at it from another angle, it's outrageously new. That dialogue makes this building not just about art and architecture but about Christianity itself and its traditions.

Suggested Reading

Faudi, *The Temple of the Sagrada Família*. This is essentially a history of the building of Sagrada Família, and it is a good place to begin a further examination of the church of Gaudí and his successors.

Basilica de la Sagrada Família, http://www.sagradafamilia.cat/sf-eng/mapaweb.php. There are innumerable links on this website with much good information and a virtual tour.

Questions to Consider

1. What do you think of what Gaudí and his successors at Sagrada Família did to transform the Gothic style into an expression of modern Christianity in Barcelona?

2. Most tourists appear not to act reverently while in La Sagrada Família. What does that say about the building as a religious edifice and about ways that modern people think of what a church should look like?

La Sagrada Família.

Incarnation portal by Antoni Gaudí.

Presentation in the temple.

Flight into Egypt.

Floor with Palm Sunday procession.

Christ at the Last Supper.

Interior of La Sagrada Família, approaching the high altar.

Crucifixion.

Iceland's Hallgrímskirkja
Lecture 23

W e've looked at a 20th-century church, albeit a rather traditional one, in Washington, DC. We have also looked at a 20th- and 21st-century church in Barcelona. In this lecture, we're moving to Iceland, to the city of Reykjavik, in particular. There, we'll see another 20th-century church that represents another expression of Christianity in the modern world, partly because it's in Iceland and partly because it is a Lutheran rather than a Catholic church.

Most people would probably imagine a typical Icelandic Lutheran church as similar to a typical American church. But the Hallgrímskirkja is quite different. It is built on a hill that dominates Reykjavik, and it is by far the largest church in Iceland. In a sense, it seems to be becoming to Iceland what the National Cathedral is to America. That is, it embodies central elements of the nation and its character.

The Hallgrímskirkja was commissioned in the 1930s by the Icelandic government to an architect named Guojon Samuelsson. It was named for an important religious and cultural figure in Iceland, Hallgrímur Pétursson. He lived in the 17th century and wrote a series of 50 hymns about the Passion of Christ. Those hymns have continued to influence the culture generally and the Christianity of Iceland a great deal. They are still sung, of course, and are sometimes memorized by schoolchildren. The hymns have become part and parcel of the culture of the Icelandic people, and both the words and the themes of the hymns are incorporated into the Hallgrímskirkja.

Although the church looks very modern, it is, ultimately, built in the form of a Gothic basilica. One of its most memorable features is its relationship to the landscape of Iceland: Both the church and the land are stark yet punctuated by bits of color. In its simplicity, the church is also an expression of the Lutheran faith and the person to whom it is dedicated. On the door to the church, one of Pétursson's hymns reminds visitors to avoid hypocrisy and ostentation, underlining the central theme of Lutheran theology: that we all depend on God's grace and mercy.

Suggested Reading

There is essentially no literature in English about the Hallgrímskirkja except for four pages of a multilingual guide to the church sold at the church gift shop. The church's website has no photographs and is only in Icelandic. Although quite brief, the website *Sacred Destinations*, "Hallgrimskirkja, Reykjavik" (http://www.sacred-destinations.com/iceland/reykjavik-hallgrimskirkja) contains some useful material and a few photographs.

Questions to Consider

1. The Hallgrímskirkja in real ways is a reflection of Iceland's history and geography. How is such a concept for a church compatible with the universality of the Christian message?

2. Does the Hallgrímskirkja lose some of its importance as a place of worship because it is made out of poured and unfinished concrete rather than the more traditional stone, of which Iceland has a great deal?

Hallgrímskirkja.

Central tower.

155

Interior of Hallgrímskirkja.

Altar.

Statue of Leif Erikson.

Detail of window.

Christ after his baptism.

Two Churches in Seoul, Korea
Lecture 24

I t's appropriate at the end of this course that we turn to Asia, which is essentially where we began. Recall that Jesus lived on the continent of Asia and, except for the trip to Egypt when he was an infant, never left Asia. Further, the first church we looked at in detail, the Church of the Holy Sepulchre, was in Asia, and we've been in Asia for churches in Armenia and Georgia. But in this lecture, we shift to the other side of the world's largest continent and take a look at East Asia, focusing on two modern churches in Seoul, Korea.

Christianity has been present outside of the Holy Land for a long time in Asia—and not just in Armenia and Georgia. There is some credible evidence and a wide belief that the apostle Thomas brought Christianity to India. We have a stone document from the city of Shiyan in China dated 781 that testifies to a Christian community there. There were Franciscans who came to East Asia in the 13th century and stayed for a time in Beijing. And in fact, the mother of one of the great Mongol rulers, Kublai Khan, was a Christian, although not a Catholic or an Orthodox Christian. The Jesuits, Franciscans, and others came in the 16th century. Although they flourished for a while in India and China, ultimately, they converted relatively few people. Thus, it is really only in the 18th through 20th centuries that Christianity has become an important presence in South and East Asia. In this lecture, we'll look at two churches in Seoul that seem to embody the recent advent of Christianity in Asia, combining elements of Christianity and modern European art with a traditional Korean approach to holy places.

These churches—one Catholic, Bulgwang-dong, and one Protestant, Kyungdong—were both designed by a famous Korean architect named Kim Swoo Geun. As we'll see, both churches are stark because they are meant to be reminders of martyrdom. Christianity didn't really begin in Korea until the 19th century, and many Koreans who became Christian, as well as the Western missionaries who brought Christianity, were martyred in the 19th century and at the beginning of the 20th. These churches commemorate those who were willing to be Christians at the risk of being martyred.

Throughout this course, we've visited about 20 countries and covered some 1,700 years of history. How can we sum up the experience of looking at some of the world's greatest churches? One obvious thing we can note is that we've seen extraordinary diversity, from the first basilicas in Rome or Hagia Sophia to La Sagrada Família or the Korean churches in this lecture. But at the same time, there is a certain unity to Christianity. All Christians believe certain things, despite the fact that they worship in very different spaces. Christian spaces are designed to say something about particular forms of Christianity and something about the cultures into which Christianity has been introduced. In this sense, Kim Swoo Geun did something similar to what other church architects have done throughout history, that is, introduced a space for Christianity that borrows from both within and outside of the Christian tradition.

We have also seen a kind of metaphor for the whole of Christian history in this course. Aristotle, for example, does not just appear on a building in Siena; he is essential to the writings of St. Thomas Aquinas. Plato is not only painted in a Romanian monastery but vital to the development of the Christian thought of St. Augustine. Thus, we have taken a journey literally around the world and metaphorically through 2,000 years of Christian tradition. We've seen how it evolved, how it is unique, and how and why it maintains its unity.

Suggested Reading

There is nothing in print in English and hardly anything in Korean about the churches of Kim Swoo Geun.

Koehler, "In Search of Kim Swoo-geun," http://www.rjkoehler. com/2007/01/03/in-search-of-kim-swoo-geun/. Here, you can grasp the range of work of Kim Swoo Geun and see a photograph of a church he designed in the city of Masan.

1. As we move from neo-Gothic churches in East Asia to the churches of Kim Swoo Geun, how can we understand the larger issue of the enculturation of Christianity in Asia?

2. It is clear that the two churches of Kim Swoo Geun are stark and emphasize the suffering of Christ. What elements of those churches celebrate hope and Christ's triumph over death?

Bulgwang-dong Catholic Church, Seoul.

Courtesy of Professor William R. Cook.

Crosses, Bulgwang-dong Catholic Church.

Devotion to the Sacred Heart of Jesus.

Station XI, Christ nailed to the Cross.

Interior of Bulgwang-dong.

Kyungdong Presbyterian Church, Seoul.

마주치는 기쁨
이경재

Statue at Kyungdong.

Courtesy of Professor William R. Cook.

Interior of Kyungdong.

Glossary

aedicule: A room or structure used as a shrine.

ambo: A raised stand for reading the Gospel or the Epistle.

apse: A semicircular area of a church on the east end, where the altar is; usually vaulted.

baldacchino: A canopy or similar structure erected over a sacred object or space, such as an altar or a tomb.

baroque: A style of art and architecture from the 17th and 18th centuries; characterized by heavy ornamentation.

barrel vault: A rounded stone vault over a space, often quite a long one.

basilica: Essentially, a rectangle with a rounded side on one of the two short sides. Originally, this building form was used for financial, judicial, or business purposes in the Roman Empire. The form was adapted by early Christians for their places of worship.

buttress: An exterior structure built against a wall to support an arch or a roof.

capital: The top of a column or pilaster.

cathedra: The chair or throne of a bishop.

fresco: Method of painting on plaster, usually done on walls.

gavit: A pass-through space containing tombs in Armenian church architecture.

groin vault: A vault produced where two barrel vaults intersect.

iconostasis: In a Greek church, a barrier between the area that most of the church occupies and the area where the altar is.

khachkar: Armenian cross stone.

mihrab: A prayer niche facing Mecca in a mosque.

misericord: Projection from the bottom of a church seat to provide support while standing during services.

narthex: A narrow enclosed porch at the entrance of a church.

nave: The central aisle in a church.

pilaster: A flat, shallow column that projects slightly out from the wall on which it is built.

reredos: A screen or wall behind an altar.

rococo: A light, playful style of art and architecture, popular in the 18th century and characterized by curving lines and ornate decoration.

sacristy: Room housing sacred vessels and vestments; where priests vest for the mass.

Solomonic column: A column with a spiral or corkscrew-shaped shaft.

transept: The shorter arms of a cross-shaped church.

transverse arch: Supporting arch that runs from side to side across the vaulting.

tympanum: The space between the lintel of a doorway and the arch above; often contains sculpture.

Bibliography

Print Resources

Anker, Leif, and Jiri Havran. *The Norwegian Stave Churches.* Oslo: ARFO, 2005. A well-illustrated church-by-church introduction to the 29 remaining (in whole or part) of the original 1,000 or so stave churches.

Batistoni, Milena. *A Guide to Lalibela.* Addis Ababa, Ethiopia: Arada Books, 2012. A good description of the churches and good photographs.

Biddle, Martin, Gideon Avni, Jon Seligman, and Tamar Winter. *The Church of the Holy Sepulchre.* New York: Rizzoli, 2000. A lucid untangling of the complex history, layout, and liturgy of the Church of the Holy Sepulchre, with beautiful photography throughout.

Binns, John. *An Introduction to the Christian Orthodox Churches.* Cambridge: Cambridge University Press, 2002. This introduction to Orthodoxy provides important contexts for understanding Orthodox churches from Istanbul to Ethiopia to Armenia.

Brumfield, William. *A History of Russian Architecture.* Seattle: University of Washington Press, 2004. This broad survey contains good chapters about the monasteries of medieval Russia and about churches in the Kremlin of Moscow.

Caciorgna, Marilena. *Virginis Templum: Cathedral, Crypt, Baptistery.* Livorno, Italy: Sillabe, 2013. This guidebook examines all parts of the cathedral complex in Siena and has many good photographs.

Caravan, Jill. *American Country Churches: A Pictorial History.* Philadelphia: Courage Books, 1996. The title tells the subject of this well-illustrated volume.

Carli, Enzo. *Siena Cathedral and the Cathedral Museum.* Milan: Scala, 1999. Carli was in charge of the cathedral for many years, and this book reflects his years of study. The section about the museum looks at the great altarpiece, the *Maestà* of Duccio.

Castijon, Rafael. *La Mezquita Aljama de Cordoba English: The Mosque of Cordoba*. Madrid: Editorial Everest, 1973. A useful introduction and guide to this multilayered building,

Crook, John. *Winchester Cathedral*. Andover, UK: Pitkin Pictorials, 1990. A short introductory guidebook with an excellent and highly detailed floor plan, photographs, and illustrations.

Dawson, Victoria, and Erik Vochinsky. *Washington National Cathedral Guidebook*. Washington, DC: Washington National Cathedral, 2007. With good diagrams and wonderful photos, this resource serves as both a guide and an introduction to the National Cathedral.

Donnelly, Marian C. *Architecture in the Scandinavian Countries*. Cambridge, MA: MIT Press, 1991. A sweeping look at Scandinavian architecture; the second chapter deals with medieval buildings, including stave churches. Not the easiest of reading but worth some struggle.

Donovan, Claire. *The Winchester Bible*. London: The British Library, 1993. One reason we looked at Winchester Cathedral was to examine one of the great manuscripts of the Middle Ages. This short work introduces the Winchester Bible handsomely.

Elo-Valente, Maarit. *Bucovina: A Travel Guide to Romania's Region of Painted Monasteries*. Helsinki, Finland: Metaneira, 2005. The definitive guide, with photos and descriptions, to the monasteries of Moldavia. Note that Bucovina is the part of Moldavia where the monasteries are located.

Fallen, Anne-Catherine, ed. *Washington National Cathedral*. Washington, DC: Washington National Cathedral, 1995. Here is an unusually lengthy guidebook, rich enough in detail to warrant the inclusion of a thorough glossary of architectural terms. Includes maps, diagrams, and spectacular photographs.

Faudi, Jordi. *The Temple of the Sagrada Familia*. Barcelona: Ediciones Palacios y Museos, 2011. With useful information about Gaudí, this is a comprehensive guide to Sagrada Família.

Fazio, Michael, Marian Moffett, and Lauren Wodehouse. *A World History of Architecture*. 2nd ed. New York: McGraw-Hill, 2008. This book is an impressive and well-illustrated resource that surveys global architecture from prehistoric settlements to skyscrapers and, thus, deals with many of the movements and churches highlighted in this course.

Frankl, Paul. *Gothic Architecture*. New Haven: Yale University Press, 2001. Frankl does not go building by building but period by period and feature by feature. This book is useful for studying Chartres, Winchester, and Siena cathedrals.

Freely, John, and Ahmet Cakmak. *Byzantine Monuments of Istanbul*. Cambridge: Cambridge University Press, 2004. These scholars have written a detailed but readable catalogue of medieval buildings remaining in Istanbul. The section on Hagia Sophia is excellent, as is the piece on SS. Sergius and Bacchus. Includes decent black-and-white photos.

Hamilton, George Heard. *Art and Architecture of Russia*. 3rd ed. New York: Penguin, 1983. A dense but rewarding study of a millennium's worth of Russian building and decoration, with emphasis on political and social context. It contains many photographs, illustrations, and floor plans.

Harada, Takeko, ed. *The Book of Ahtamar Reliefs*. Istanbul: A. Turizm Yayınları, 2003. A rare work in English on Armenian churches; good text and excellent photos describing the Church of the Holy Cross.

Harmel, Jean-Regis. "The Tympanum of Conques in Detail." Montpellier: JF/Impression, 2012. This brief pamphlet is a wonderful guide to the iconography of the tympanum of Conques.

Johnston, Francis. *The Wonder of Guadalupe*. Charlotte, NC: TAN, 1993. A survey of the story of Juan Diego and the shrine of Our Lady of Guadalupe.

Katzenellenbogen, Adolf. *The Sculptural Program of Chartres Cathedral: Christ, Mary, Ecclesia.* Baltimore, MD: Johns Hopkins University Press, 1959. This book is deservedly a classic study of the iconography of Chartres Cathedral.

Kendig, Robert. *The Washington National Cathedral: The Bible in Stone.* McLean, VA: EPM Publications, 1995. A useful book with stories about the cathedral's construction and, as the title suggests, about the decorations and how to interpret them.

Kirchmeir, Georg, and Margret Hasenmuller. *The Wies: The Pilgrimage Church of the "Scourged Saviour."* Lechbruck, Germany: Verlag Wilhelm Kienberger, 1992. Quite a good introduction to the Wieskirche, with photographs and diagrams.

Kostof, Spiro. *Caves of God: Cappadocia and Its Churches.* New York: Oxford University Press, 1989. A treatment of the rock-cut churches of Cappadocia, at once readable and meticulous. Kostof's passion for his subject is infectious.

Krautheimer, Richard. *Early Christian and Byzantine Architecture.* 4th ed. New York: Penguin, 1986. Krautheimer's book is a standard work on early Christian architecture. It deals with the churches mentioned in Lecture 1 and provides a context for them

Male, Emile. *The Gothic Image: Religious Art in France of the Thirteenth Century.* New York: Harper, 1972. Looking broadly at Gothic art in France, this wonderful book is a great help in understanding Chartres Cathedral.

Menocal, Maria Rosa. *The Ornament of the World: How Muslims, Jews, and Christians Created a Culture of Tolerance in Medieval Spain.* New York: Back Bay Books, 2003. This book sets a broad and deep context for the history of the Mosque-Cathedral of Córdoba.

Mercier, Jacques, and Claude Lepage. *Lalibela: Wonder of Ethiopia: The Monolithic Churches and Their Treasures.* London: Paul Holberton, 2012.

Bibliography

Not the most readable book but quite a thorough study of the churches. Lavishly illustrated.

Miller, Malcolm. *Chartres Cathedral.* New York: Riverside Book Company, 1997. Malcolm Miller has a lifelong love affair with Chartres Cathedral, and his tours are legendary. This book and everything Miller has written is insightful.

————. *Chartres Cathedral: Medieval Masterpieces in Stained Glass and Sculpture.* London: Pitkin Guides, 1994.

Montiel, Martin Castellanos. *Metropolitan Cathedral of Mexico City.* Mexico City: Octavio Antonio Colmenares y Vargas, 2012. Not the most readable book, but it contains information about the Cathedral of Mexico City that is not available in English anywhere else.

Morris, Colin. *The Sepulchre of Christ and the Medieval West.* Oxford: Oxford University Press, 2005. A scholarly yet readable book about the Holy Sepulchre and how it was understood in the West in the Middle Ages; written by a distinguished medievalist.

Morrissey, Jake. *The Genius in the Design: Bernini, Borromini, and the Rivalry That Transformed Rome.* New York: Harper, 2006. Parts of this book discuss Bernini's work on St. Peter's, including the great piazza in front of it.

Norberg-Schulz, Christian. *Nightlands: Nordic Building.* Cambridge, MA: MIT Press, 1996. An engaging meditation on the meaning and singularity of Nordic architecture, with emphasis on the importance of topography and climate to the character of the built form. Chapter 4 deals with stave churches.

Ogden, Alan. *Revelations of Byzantium: The Monasteries and Painted Churches of Northern Moldavia.* Iasi, Romania: The Center for Romanian Studies, 2002. Ogden introduces the historical context, architecture, and art of the Moldavian monasteries. The book includes extensive diagrams, much photography, and a section with short studies of many of the individual sites.

Oney, Gonul. *The Church of Akdamar.* Ankara, Turkey: Ministry of Culture Publications, 1990. A brief but useful description and explanation of an important Armenian church; it is particularly good in examining the exterior sculpture.

Pétursson, Hallgrímur. *The Passion Hymns of Iceland, Being Translations from the Passion-Hymns of Hallgrim Petursson and from the Hymns of the Modern Icelandic Hymn Book.* Toronto: University of Toronto Press, 2011. One volume in a large series containing English translations of the hymns that are the inspiration for the Hallgrímskirkja in Reykjavik.

Rodley, Lyn. *Cave Monasteries of Byzantine Cappadocia.* Cambridge: Cambridge University Press, 1985. The photos are in black and white, and the author is more interested in the buildings than in the decoration. Still, this book is thorough and, thus, useful.

Roffey, Simon. *Chantry Chapels and Medieval Strategies for the Afterlife.* Abingdon, UK: The History Press, 2008. This will serve as an introduction to the chantry chapels at Winchester Cathedral discussed in Lecture 15.

Santi, Bruno. *The Marble Pavement of the Cathedral of Siena.* Milan: Scala, 1982. Take the opportunity to learn from this book about the unique floor of Siena's cathedral.

Sciortino, Lisa. *The Cathedral of Monreale.* San Vendemiano, Italy: Simie Books, 2012. A quite good and well-illustrated introduction to Monreale's cathedral.

Scotti, R. A. *Basilica: The Splendor and the Scandal: Building St. Peter's.* New York: Plume, 2007. A popular book and an easy and fascinating read that gives a good context for and history of the building of the world's largest church.

Sheingorn, Pamela. *The Book of Sainte Foy.* Philadelphia: University of Pennsylvania Press, 1995. This interesting translation with commentary of a medieval text about Sainte Foy and her miracles is useful for understanding the importance of pilgrimage to Sainte Foy and, hence, to the building and decoration of the splendid abbey at Conques.

Soltes, Oli, ed. *National Treasures of Georgia: Art and Civilization through the* Ages. London: Philip Wilson, 2003. Part IV of this book contains important essays about the art of medieval Georgia, including architecture and painting.

Statzger, Alfons. *Wies Church: A Place of Pilgrimage near Steingaden, Upper Bavaria.* Augsburg, Germany: Die Brigg, 1953. An older, short text, this is nevertheless a methodical and efficient treatment of the history, architecture, and decoration of the Weis Church, with illustrations and black-and-white photography. This resource is available in full online at www. openlibrary.org , a digital lending library for which registration is free.

Sumption, Jonathan. *The Age of Pilgrimage: The Medieval Journey to God.* Mahwah, NJ: Hiddenspring Books, 2003. A good introduction to medieval pilgrimage; provides useful information and context for the Holy Sepulchre, Rome, and Conques.

Wallace, William. *Michelangelo: The Artist, His Work and His Times.* Cambridge: Cambridge University Press, 2011. One section of this most impressive biography focuses on Michelangelo's contribution to St. Peter's.

Winchester Cathedral. Andover, UK: Pitkin Publishing, 2012. A good guide to the cathedral with a useful floor plan and good photographs.

Online Resources (listed by lecture)

Lecture 1
Fletcher, Adrian. "The Major Basilica of Santa Maria Maggiore: Triumphal Arch Mosaics." http://www.paradoxplace.com/Perspectives/Rome%20 &%20Central%20Italy/Rome/Rome_Churches/Santa_Maria_Maggiore/ Santa_Maria_Maggiore_Triumphal_Arch/Santa_Maria_Maggiore_ Mosaics_T.htm. This website shows all of the New Testament mosaics in Santa Maria Maggiore in Rome from the 5th century.

Witcombe, Christopher L. C. E. *Art History Resources*. http://arthistoryresources.net/ARTHearlychristian.html#Top. Includes links to photos and diagrams of many early Christian churches.

Lecture 2
Gerusalemme San Salvatore Convento Francescano St. Saviour's Monastery. *Holy Sepulchre*. http://www.holysepulchre.custodia.org. A glossy resource featuring three-dimensional videos and diagrams of the evolution and layout of the Church of the Holy Sepulchre.

Sacred Destinations. "Church of the Holy Sepulchre, Jerusalem." http://www.sacred-destinations.com/israel/jerusalem-church-of-holy-sepulchre. A useful site with both text and images.

Lecture 3
Hagia Sophia. http://www.3dmekanlar.com/en/hagia-sophia.html. Enjoy a virtual tour of this most splendid building, soon to celebrate its 1,500[th] anniversary.

Lecture 4
Turkish Heritage Travel. *Goreme Open-Air Museum*. http://www.goreme. com/goreme-open-air-museum.php. This site gives a brief but useful introduction to the churches and other ancient and medieval structures of Cappadocia.

Lecture 5
Moscow.Info, Inc. *Churches of the Kremlin*. http://www.moscow.info/kremlin/churches/index.aspx. Includes descriptions of and information about all the churches in Moscow's Kremlin.

Lecture 6
Art of the Fresco: Romania's Painted Monasteries. http://romania-monastery.info/. An interesting article about the history and preservation of fresco painting in Romania.

Lecture 7

Haykland.com. "The Amazing Blend of Nature and Ancient Churches." http://www.haykland.com/monuments.php. A brief but rather complete catalogue of surviving Armenian monastic churches.

Moscow.Info, Inc. *Churches of the Kremlin.* http://www.moscow.info/ kremlin/churches/index.aspx. Includes descriptions of and information about all the churches in Moscow's Kremlin.

Lecture 8

Saints Peter and Paul Serbian Orthodox Church. "Monasteries and Churches in Georgia." http://atlantaserbs.com/learnmore/monasteries and towns/ Gruzija.htm. A useful list with descriptions and photos of the most important surviving Georgian monasteries.

Lecture 9

Barnett, Errol. "Rock Churches of Lalibela, the Jerusalem of Ethiopia." www.cnn.com/2013/06/27/travel/rock-churches-lalibela-ethiopia/. *CNN looked at Lalibela, and this website includes three interesting videos largely made on site.*

Lecture 10

Donadio, Rachel. "Name Debate Echoes an Old Clash of Faiths." *The New York Times.* http://www.nytimes.com/2010/11/05/world/europe/05cordoba. html?pagewanted=all&_r=0. An article from a few years ago about controversies today regarding the Cathedral of Córdoba and its Muslim origin.

Reed, Tony. "Photo Album: Mosque-Cathedral of Cordoba, Spain." http:// www.infocordoba.com/spain/andalusia/cordoba/photos/mosque_2/index. htm. A very nice and rather substantial photo collection of the Mosque-Cathedral of Córdoba.

Santa Iglesia Catedral de Córdoba. http://www.catedraldecordoba.es. The official website of the Cathedral of Córdoba boasts a surfeit of photography and an interactive floor plan. Information on history, design, and chapels is presented in relatively brief flurries. The English-language version of the site can be accessed by clicking on the Union Jack in the upper right corner of the homepage.

Lecture 11
Innovation Norway. *Visitnorway.com*. "Stave Churches." http://www. visitnorway.com/us/About-Norway/History/Stave-churches/. This site offers a look at all of the surviving stave churches.

Jensenius, Jergen H. *Stavkirke.info*. http://www.stavkirke.info/english. Though much of this site is in Norwegian, an English-language section features an introduction to the planning and design of the medieval stave churches. Also included are a bibliography and noteworthy article-by-article summaries of the relevant scholarship, most of which is of Norwegian origin.

Lecture 12
Catedral de Santiago. "Pilgrim's Welcome Office." http://peregrinossantiago. es/eng/. The official website for modern pilgrims walking to Santiago de Compostela.

Office de Tourisme, Conques. "The Tympanum of the Last Judgment." http://www.tourisme-conques.fr/en/histoire-patrimoine/eglise-abbatiale/ tympan-jugement-dernier.php. This site provides a detailed description and photos of the tympanum.

Lecture 13
Planetware. "Monreale Cathedral." http://www.planetware.com/monreale/ monreale-cathedral-i-si-monct.htm. Includes a useful diagram of Monreale Cathedral plus a very good map of the mosaics on the walls.

Lecture 14
Chartres Cathedral. http://www.medievalart.org.uk/chartres/Chartres_ default.htm. A great website to learn about the windows, with diagrams and photos of each one.

Lecture 15

Winchester Cathedral. http://winchester-cathedral.org.uk/gallery/?album= 1&gallery=11. Winchester Cathedral's website has links to many of the most interesting features of the cathedral, including the Winchester Bible.

Lecture 16

Olga's Gallery. "Duccio di Buoninsegna." http://www.abcgallery.com/D/ duccio/maesta.html. From this website, you can look at each detail of Duccio's great altarpiece of 1311, the *Maestà*.

Lecture 17

Saintpetersbasilica.org. http:// www.saintpetersbasilica.org/. The official website of St. Peter's has an almost infinite number of resources, even a tour by Sister Wendy of PBS fame.

Lecture 18

Wieskirche. http://www.wieskirche.de/eframset.htm. The Wieskirche's website includes a historical outline, a useful chronology, and interactive panoramic views of the interior.

Lecture 19

Guardian Angel. "Las Lajas Cathedral." http://www.guardianangel.in/ ga/192-GuardianStory-Las-Lajas-Cathedral.html. A source for some historical information about Las Lajas plus some decent photographs.

"Tour Virtual: La Compañía de Jesús." http://www.qpqweb.com/index. php?option=com content&view=article&id=55&Itemid=68. A gorgeous, panoramic virtual tour of La Compañía in Quito is available here. The website is in Spanish but the mechanics of the tour are intuitive.

Lecture 20

The Basilica of Guadalupe. http://www.sancta.org/basilica.html. There are several links on this website, including one to a virtual visit to the shrine of Guadalupe; there is also some history.

Mexico City-Guide.com. "Metropolitan Cathedral." http://www.mexicocity-guide.com/attractions/cathedral%20.htm. A brief but helpful introduction to Mexico City's cathedral can be found here.

Mexico City Metropolitan Cathedral. http://www.infosources.org/what_is/Mexico_City_Metropolitan_Cathedral.html. For examining the history and the various elements of the Cathedral of Mexico City, this is quite a useful site.

Lecture 21
First Congregational Church of Guilford, CT. http://www.firstchurchguilford.org. The official website of the First Church of Guilford, Connecticut, with a short introduction to its history and a number of links to other resources for deeper reading.

Washington National Cathedral. "Online and Virtual Tours." http://www.nationalcathedral.org/visit/onlineTours.shtml. The Washington National Cathedral's website features some of the highest-quality virtual tours available for a place of worship, from narrated video tours to "high-impact" panoramas with a zoom function that allows for the inspection of details hidden even to the cathedral's physical visitors.

Wikimedia Commons. "Stained Glass Windows of the Washington National Cathedral." http://commons.wikimedia.org/wiki/Category:Stained_glass_windows_of_the_Washington_National_Cathedral. This site allows you to look at many of the stained-glass windows and provides brief explanations.

Lecture 22
Basilica de la Sagrada Família. http://www.sagradafamilia.cat/sf-eng/mapaweb.php. Quite thorough, this website gives visitors a large number of links from which to learn about Gaudí and his church, Sagrada Família.

Lecture 23
Nordic Adventure Travel. "Hallgrim's Church." http://www.nat.is/Churches/hallgrim%27s_church_rvik.htm. Because there is very little in English about the Hallgrimskirkja, this site is useful.

Sacred Destinations. "Hallgrimskirkja, Reykjavik." http://www.sacred-destinations.com/iceland/reykjavik-hallgrimskirkja. There is not much information on this website, but it is about all that is available in English about the Hallgrimskirkja.

Lecture 24
Koehler, Robert. "In Search of Kim Swoo-geun." http://www.rjkoehler.com/2007/01/03/in-search-of-kim-swoo-geun/. This site provides a look at some of the architectural achievements of Kin Swoo Geun, including the Kyungdong Presbyterian Church and an earlier church of his in the city of Masan.

Notes